A COLD CLEAR DAY

A COLD CLEAR DAY

THE ATHLETIC BIOGRAPHY OF
BUDDY EDELEN

WRITTEN BY
FRANK MURPHY
POSTSCRIPT BY
HAL HIGDON

WINDSPRINT
PRESS
KANSAS CITY

For information, address:
Wind Sprint Press
P.O. Box 412074
Kansas City, Missouri 64141

Library of Congress Cataloging in Publication Data
Murphy, Frank (Frank J.), 1952-
A cold clear day: the athletic biography of Buddy Edelen
written by Frank Murphy. -- 1st ed.
    p. cm.
Includes bibliographical references.
1. Edelen, Buddy, 1937-   . 2. Runners (Sports) -- United States --
Biography. 3. Marathon running. I. Title.
    GV1061.15.E34M87   1991
    796.42'092--dc20   91-9113
    [B]   CIP

Book design by Susan Ng

FIRST EDITION

ISBN 0-9629243-0-X

To Mary

PREFACE

Buddy Edelen was a marathoner. Although he was an American, he did his best running in England in the early 1960s, at a time when England was redefining itself. With its empire gone and with an economy racked by debt and labor unrest following World War II, England was proving that it could remain a world power by energy alone. In music, in fashion, in theater, in attitude itself, the island, now an outlet unto itself, imploded. Athletics, or track and field as it is called in the United States, had a place in England's renewal.

In the period immediately after the war, holdovers like Sydney Wooderson, Tom Richards and Jack Holden enjoyed final triumphs over age and dislocation. In time, young runners appeared. Roger Bannister, Chris Chataway and Chris Brasher, between them and individually, produced the first sub four-minute mile; an even faster mile in Bannister's epic confrontation with John Landy in the 1954 British Empire Games; a furious chase down the backstretch against Emil Zatopek in Helsinki's 1952 Olympic 5,000-meter final; a world 5,000-meter record against Vladimir Kuts at the floodlit grounds of London's White City, and an Olympic championship steeplechase in Melbourne, 1956. With the three friends came Jim Peters, the first marathoner to go under 2 hours, 20 minutes (2:20), and Gordon Pirie, who proved both the value and the expense of concentrated effort by setting world records at 3,000 and 5,000 meters before taking a heroic beating from Kuts over 10,000 meters in the 1956 Olympic Games. Add to the list literally dozens of names which crowded athletics reports from the period just after the war and into the 1960s, names like Tulloh and Ibbotson, Freddie Green, Stan Cox, Mike Rawson and Derek Johnson, Brian Hewson, Martin Hyman, Mel Batty, Brian Kilby and Basil Heatley and you have an England in which running was king.

Buddy Edelen was a good runner by American standards when he went to England in 1960, but he was not then and never would be a stylist. He did not have the quick, even patter of Bikila; the pulling stride of Ron Hill; or the characteristic float of Frank Shorter, Edelen's heir to the American marathon. Nor could Buddy be compared to Zatopek, the classic "ugly" runner, who nonetheless maintained an even stride beneath his clutching, agonized carriage. Rather, Buddy's stride was short, staccato, brisk in the most generous estimations-- like a chicken pecking the ground, in the most unkind. Ultimately, however, the form was insignificant. At most it was the criterion by which unknowing people judged talent. The drive train to any runner is the mind, not the stylized movement of arms and legs. In this more important regard, Buddy had what he needed.

It is occasionally said in athletics, in reference to the fragility of talent, that to train hard or to compete with frequency is to drive nails with a Stradivarius. Buddy Edelen, having no Stradivarius, pounded nails without compunction. In doing so, this American with the curious stride ran a marathon in 1963 faster than any man ever had. It was the first time since 1925 that an American had held that distinction.

This is the story of that marathon and the man who ran it.

*Marathon running is
a terrible experience --
monotonous, heavy, and exhausting.*

Veikko Karvonen
1954 European and Boston Marathon Champion

CHAPTER ONE

Conviction is the present possession of one's own life.
Michelstaedter

The Thames River begins at Thameshead, as the name implies, although the stream there is sometimes dry, or it begins at Seven Springs, the furthest point of any headstream from the mouth. From both locations the streams converge just above Cricklade and move north and east toward Oxford, joined enroute by Coln, Windrush, Evenlode and by the other waters trailing down the southeast slope of the Cotswolds. At Oxford, the Thames is joined by its principal tributary, the Cherwell, which flows south from a source in the Northampton uplands. Below Oxford, the river cuts through the low ridge of the Oxford Heights, crosses from clay to chalk at Wallingford, breaks occasionally into several parts, isolates islands along the way and adds tributaries from the Vales of Aylesbury and White Horse. With new strength it courses through the chalk escarpment in the Goring Gap and into the lower basin. After it passes Reading, the Thames is three sides of a square to the north--Henley, Marlow and Maidenhead-- before approaching the riverside towns of Windsor, Eton and Slough, then Staines, Walton, Hampton, Kingston and Teddington. Entering London, the river is bound first by gravel-covered terraces and then, in the city proper, by 3 1/2 miles of embankment, a feat of Victorian engineering that reclaimed 32 acres of land at the temporary expense of the river's natural width and depth. Leaving London, England's longest river slides quietly under the many road and rail bridges, passes the Docks and finally, as if in recompense for the artificial constraint of London, broadens to an estuary as it moves east. At its widest point, the Thames Estuary stetches 5 1/2 miles across, measured from Shoeburyness to Sheerness. Marked by the Nore lighthouse, it releases into the North Sea, from which it is now indistinguishable.

. .

The day was December 10, 1963, a clear, cold day with temperatures in the high 30s and wind from the east at 12 miles per hour. The town was Westcliffe-on-Sea, Essex, a fading holiday resort 30 miles east of London on the Thames Estuary. Buddy Edelen's flat, for which he paid the equivalent of seven dollars a week, was one room with one window on the second floor of a building he shared with his landlord. The room was furnished with a coin-operated heater, a cot, a portable dresser, a wooden chair, a transistor radio, a small stove and a clutter of trophies. It had no refrigerator, because Buddy considered himself a compulsive eater and didn't want food around, and it had no television, because Buddy could not afford one and, in any event, had no time to use it. The available bathroom, equipped with a tub but no shower, was outside the door and to the right of the stairway.

Buddy was awake at 7 from eight fitful hours of sleep, made worse by the cold and the inadequacy of the heating, an imposed economy. Immediately he checked his pulse. It was 42 beats per minute, which was higher than the 38 he sometimes recorded but significantly lower than the pulse rate of 72 other people considered normal. He next stepped gingerly over to the scale. His weight was 140 pounds, some 10 pounds less than when he first arrived in England. At 5 feet 10 inches, that weight wizened his face and angulated his body, but it left him just enough muscle, bone and tendon to run on, with not an ounce of fat to hold him back.

Having verified a runner's vital signs, Buddy put on several layers of shirts and sweats, each one of which clashed colorfully with the one above and below it, and added shorts. The shorts, worn and stretched and too large to begin with, were pinned in place along his hips. A second pin, also attached to the shorts, held the key to the flat. Finally he pulled on his Tiger running shoes, the newest sensation from Japan when he got them, but long since flat and lifeless from wear.

By now an unusual sight in any neighborhood except this one, which was accustomed to him, Buddy Edelen left the flat and jogged down to the corner market, where he got a daily paper. He returned home and read the paper over coffee before going back down the stairs and into the street. He paused only momentarily before breaking into a run, turning left toward the Estuary and then right onto the High Road. Although the wind was against him and the course was uphill, Buddy ran hard, accelerating throughout. Precisely 4 1/2 miles later, he arrived at the King John Modern Secondary School, where he was employed as a teacher for the equivalent of $150 dollars per month. After a quick shower, he changed into the suit and tie he left there the evening before and had a breakfast of rye crisp, honey, grapefruit and more coffee. With that, the working day could begin.

Because he had no academic specialty, Buddy taught everything from history to home economics. He drew the line only at the course called Mothercraft, for which he felt ill-prepared by nature. Whatever Buddy taught, he was a conscientious worker, well received by faculty and students alike. His headmaster, upon being asked whether Buddy's employment wasn't a preference extended as a result of his status as a world-class runner, said no, that Buddy Edelen was a good teacher and that he could teach at King John's even if he had a wooden leg. With the students, a coeducational group of young teenagers, Buddy was only occasionally forced to use the "American hit parade," a ruler good for the timely and well-directed tap. His problem in class was not discipline, it was fatigue, the natural result of running 135 miles a week as fast as possible and of racing on the weekends

Flowing ceaselessly, Buddy Edelen on the run.

Buddy taught everything from History to Home Economics.

everywhere from Hyde Park to Morocco. At mid-afternoon, he fought an inclination to nod off.

By 1963, Buddy had been in England for three years living and working like this, changing to adapt—to take the strong values of this culture as his own. The changes were most noticeable in the way he spoke. His accent retained something of the States' upper Midwest, but it blended with the phonetic devices the English use to provide diversity and distinction to a language they must otherwise find bland. Buddy was especially vulnerable to the idiom of British athletics. He trained in a "kit" with the other "chaps." Every now and then they would "bash" one. If he had a particularly good run, that would be a "burner" and if he had a bad one he would be "shattered." If he did well, it was "bloody well." Using such terms he might equally have been an American in England or an Englishman just back from an extended stay in America.

When classes ended at 3, Buddy changed back into his kit and was out the door, finding comfort in what looked an uncomfortable running form. Leaning well back on his heels and curling the right arm toward his body, his strides were quick and rhythmic, if not graceful. Buddy sometimes trained at the school yard, the King John Roller Coaster he called the track because of its many rises and falls, but today he headed home on the High Road. He ran the 4 1/2 miles at a steady pace and then added a roundabout 4 1/2 mile run to the sea front.

In the summer, the promenade at the sea front was crowded with strollers, barkers, people enjoying the breeze and concessions, all manner of people for all manner of purposes. Occasionally, when the weather was good and the crowds were thick, the holiday-makers were surprised by Buddy's routine and by the motion of his stride, and they laughed. On this winter day, Buddy was gratefully alone in the dusk.

Buddy Edelen was a long-distance runner, but he and his coach from Indiana, Fred Wilt, never forgot the ultimate value of speed. It was no good plodding, even if your race distance was 26 miles long. For these two, winter was not a dead spot in the schedule, useful only for the accumulation of slow base miles; it was the time to build speed, to raise the athlete's tempo. Buddy, who considered himself devoid of natural speed, was at the sea front this afternoon to address the issue over the length of a measured, lighted quarter-mile stretch. With nearly 14 miles of running already done in the day, he added 20 lengths of the stretch, alternating very fast quarter miles with relatively slow ones. In the cold weather, he wore several heavy sweat shirts. The extra clothing made the work harder but Buddy was unbothered. If his purpose was fitness, the extra burden of heavy clothing, harsh weather or difficult surface would only make the end result more certain.

Having run the 20th quarter mile, Buddy jogged back to his flat in darkness. Arriving home, he washed, changed clothes and then went back to the High Road. Near him, the area was crowded with small shops: magazines, newspapers, chemists, fish and chips, the fish monger. It also offered a traditional English pub, which provided warmth and conversation in the evening glow. Buddy, because his stomach would not accept solid food so soon after a hard run, because he accepted the warmth of the room and the congeniality of the company, because he enjoyed his favorite brew of Guinness stout, because he had persuaded himself that it was a rich blend of vitamins and iron recommended even for nursing mothers, and because it helped him sleep, stopped off for a pint or two at the equivalent of 47 cents each.

Although the pub is a fixture in England's social community, not much different in function from the coffee house in Vienna or the cafe in Paris, Buddy could be defensive about his presence there and his beer, however helpful it might be in moderation. He knew that people who viewed him as an example, whether in England or back home in America, would find it easy to emulate the beer he drank and somewhat more difficult to surround it with hard work, which was its context. It was the work, he would emphasize, that mattered and not the beer. He could only hope that people listened.

On this evening, as on others like it, Buddy drank the stout slowly, letting the pressures of the day fade into conversation, and then

He accepted the warmth of the room and the congeniality of the company.

he walked home, stopping only to buy an evening paper and something for dinner.

He was a solitary figure tonight, walking by the bungalows and the small shops for which England was famous, but he wasn't always so. On some nights he was a welcome guest in the homes of his running mates. On other nights he had his girlfriends. The young women might get annoyed when he left early to get some sleep so he could run in the morning, but he was, after all, an American in England. He was also young, ambitious, considered charming and handsome, coincidentally modest and prideful and a success at what he set out to do, however arcane the ambition might appear. As a result, Buddy had been close to marriage with several British girls. He loved children and the idea of a family attracted him. But that future would have to wait. As it pulled toward him, he pushed away. His life now was running and it consumed him.

Arriving at the flat, Buddy ate alone, worked briefly on the next day's lesson plan and, at last, sat down with his daily work sheet. The work sheet was a form Fred Wilt devised. Wilt was a career officer in the Federal Bureau of Investigation, but his passion was running. More particularly, his passion was training to run, and on this point his precision was legend. He had designed this work sheet in detail. On it, Buddy recorded his pulse, his weight, what he ate during the day, the weather conditions, the venue for each of his workouts, what he ran, at what pace, with what interval, with whom and, finally, his remarks. The sheets made it possible for Fred to advise Buddy despite the great physical distance between them. When Buddy collected 7 or 10 of the sheets he would mail them to Fred, waiting in Indiana. Fred would review each of the sheets and then return them with his scrawled comments, giving Buddy a nudge one way or the other, asking in turn for more speed, less speed, more distance, less distance, more work, more rest, more racing, less racing—whatever was required in a circumstance that changed by the day if not by the hour.

The diary complete, Buddy was asleep by 11, both comforted and anxious that tomorrow would be more of the same.

CHAPTER TWO

He made an exhaustive study of training methods and
form employed by the leading European distance specialists.

Citation, The Sullivan Award
1950, awarded to Fred Wilt

It is possible to argue that the development of middle-and long-distance training technique is a continuum in which the advance of one method gives way to the next in a reasonable, causative sequence. By that argument the personality of any single athlete is minimized. There are no pioneers, no moving forces, only representatives of incremental change.

In 1948 and even more remarkably in 1952, it was hard to credit such a theory in the face of Emil Zatopek. The Czechoslovakian runner appeared wholecloth, a man capable of training at stunning intensity. It was said that before the Olympic Games in 1948, in which he won a gold medal in the 10,000 meter and a silver medal in the 5,000 meter, he ran 400 meters 60 times with only a 200-meter jog between the hard runs and that he did the workout 10 days in a row. Before the 1952 Olympic Games in Helsinki, where he won gold medals in all three long-distance events, Zatopek's favorite workout was 20 times 200 meters, followed by 40 times 400 meters, followed by 20 times 200 meters.

Fred Wilt was at London in 1948 and at Helsinki in 1952 as a member of the United States Olympic teams. Close as he was to the action, it would have been easy to get lost in the personality of Emil Zatopek and to copy him, as one did original art. But Fred Wilt was an analytical sort. In time, he knew that as great as Emil Zatopek was, he was not the only one. He represented an evolutionary stage. Overpowering as Emil was, he was not born that way; he was created by hard, purposeful training. Fred Wilt believed it when Emil said: If you would beat me, find a better way to train.

· ·

"I travelled ever so casually and quietly, training for distance only and leaving speed entirely out of it," wrote long-distance champion Arthur Newton, and so, in the main, did other long distance runners before World War II. With the exception of Hannes Kolehmainen's victory in the 1920 Olympic marathon in Antwerp, at a time when Kolehmainen's better days were behind him, the major marathons in the first half of the 20th century were won by specialists. People like Thomas Hicks, Kenneth McArthur, Boughera El Ouafi and Juan Zabala won Olympic titles because they trained to run long and they did, while others similarly trained did not. It was a game for survivors.

Jim Peters was the first marathoner to inject speed with regularity into his training and therefore his racing. The kind of man he was, a tough, driving man from London's east side, Peters' methods were predictably simple and predictably harsh. He ran 11 to 13 times a week, during which he would cover between 80 and 120 miles. He ran all of it between 5 minutes and 5 minutes, 15 seconds per mile. By cutting the distance of any individual run, by running multiple daily workouts, and by doing so at a fast tempo, Peters alloyed speed and strength in a manner that had been unknown. With that, he moved the marathon record below 2 hours and 20 minutes at a time when 2 hours and 30 minutes was considered world-class running.

In the 1952 marathon in Helsinki, Peters put his speed to good use. He pulled through the 10km in 31:55 and 15km in 47:58. In prior Olympic marathons, Peters might have been alone at that pace. In Helsinki, he discovered, as much as he had done, he had not done enough. Emil Zatopek was there and Emil Zatopek was faster. While Zatopek won the Olympic title in his first marathon, Peters cramped and went out.

Fred Wilt watched Peters and Zatopek with interest. Peters was able to cut the jogging out of his program and run hard every day because he broke his running into two or three sessions a day. But Peters lacked any single long run approaching the marathon distance. Wilt accepted the value of Zatopek's extended interval workouts; they could build speed and strength. That much was obvious from Zatopek's racing and made sense physiologically. But specifically in terms of marathon running, Zatopek also lacked the long, continuous run on the road.

Fred thought that if he could combine Peters' workouts at near-race pace with hard intervals like those of Zatopek, and then add long road runs at something gradually approaching the full marathon distance, he could get even better results. In the late 1950s what he needed in order to test his conclusion was an American runner. He wanted one with sufficient experience on the track to see the necessity, indeed the very reasonableness, of running fast in order to run long— and of running long in order to run fast. And he needed a runner tough enough to make it happen.

· · ·

Fred Wilt found his man in Buddy Edelen:

"Buddy was a junior at the University of Minnesota in 1958. Minnesota is in the Big Ten athletic conference and so is Purdue University, which is located in my hometown of Lafayette, Indiana.

Buddy With Coach Jim Kelley at the University of Minnesota.

When the Big Ten held its track and field championships at Purdue in 1958, I was there, of course, interested as always in the distance events. The two-mile run was supposed to be between Buddy and Deacon Jones, a fine runner from Iowa who had been on our 1956 Olympic team as a steepler.

"Buddy had been undefeated as a high school miler in South Dakota with a best time under 4:30, which was rare in those days. As a sophomore at Minnesota, he was fourth in the Big Ten and ninth in the national meet in cross-country, and then fourth in the national collegiates over two miles on the track. He won the Big Ten cross-country meet his junior year and was fourth nationally. In the 1957-1958 school year, Buddy and Deacon traded victories. Buddy won the Big Ten cross-country meet over Deacon and Deacon returned the favor in the indoor two mile. So it would be interesting to see who got this one.

"In fact, Buddy led every step of the two miles and Deacon Jones wasn't even second. Buddy remembers the race differently than I do. It's been a lot of years for both of us, since 1958 after all, but Buddy thinks that the runner who eventually came second, Fordy Kennedy of Michigan State, Glasgow and finally Canada, passed him on the last stretch and that he had to respond late. Maybe it felt like that to Buddy, but my recollection is that Kennedy was close but never got there.

"I think Buddy confuses this meet with the cross-country championship the previous fall, in which Kennedy passed him in the last mile and Buddy had to fight very hard to win. In either event, you have to keep in mind that Fordy Kennedy was a good runner, one who would win the National Collegiate cross-country meet later in 1958, and it was to Buddy's credit that he could take him--first in cross-country and then over two miles on the track. Anyway, Buddy won the Big Ten two mile in 1958 in a conference record of 9:03. Kennedy was second and Deacon Jones came in third, although in fairness I think Deacon also won the mile for Iowa that day.

"Buddy had an unusual stride—I can remember people around me in the stands remarking about it— but I thought it was fine. Better yet was his attitude. Most people don't have the courage to lead in an important race. Buddy did. When he ran, a change came over him. You could see the amiability in him right to the time the gun sounded. Then his eyes darkened, his features flattened, his chest expanded, he stood up a little straighter. As the race progressed, he had a quality almost like meanness. He just would not let up.

"After the race I went down to visit with him. Maybe it's not something I should have done, but it felt right at the time. I waited, and when Buddy came down I talked with him for a few minutes. At that time all our runners were quitting just out of college. There was no money in the sport and a young man, no matter how talented, had to make a living, and that might not leave room for running. So I wanted to see what his attitude was, with an eye toward coaching him, although advising may be a better word for it, and more importantly just helping him stay with running after he graduated.

"Buddy was not hesitant about it. He wanted to run and, on his own account, had hoped to continue. I thought then, and I said so, that he could make our Olympic team. I don't think I mentioned what event I had in mind or what year it could happen though. I did emphasize to Buddy that the United States was no place to run the distances. This country had only isolated historical accomplishment in distance running and no environment conducive to the hard training and racing that would be required.

"I don't recall that Buddy and I had significant personal contact in the first year or so after that meeting at the Big Ten. But we did correspond, and I got to know him a little better and got some idea what he had been doing. But he still had a year of eligibility at the University of Minnesota and I did not want to interfere with that. We both recognized, however, the need to put more volume into his running. That point was emphasized at the National Collegiate track meet in 1958, when Buddy finished well back in the two mile in much slower time than at the Big Ten. He didn't have the strength to carry him through the long season.

"When you saw how he trained, you could understand the problem. Buddy's training at Minnesota didn't come to much more than 25 miles a week. I published through *Track and Field News* a book called *How They Train* in which I had the athletes describe how they prepared to race. I've got Buddy's section in front of me. You wonder how he could run near nine flat for two miles on that kind of work:

Spring training (outdoors):

Monday: 1 1/4 mile in 6:50. 880 in 2:09.
Jog and walk 10 minutes and then 5-7 times
a quarter mile in 63-64. Walk and jog 220s.

Tuesday: 20 x 220 in 29-30 seconds.
Walk and jog 3-4 minutes between each.
Mile in 5:30.

Wednesday: 10 x 440 in 61-63. Walk and jog
1 to 1 1/2 minutes after the first 7 and
2 to 2 1/2 minutes after the last 3-440s.

Thursday: Jog 1 mile. Calisthenics, a few wind
sprints. Jog one mile.

Friday and Sunday: rest.

Saturday: race.

Actually that was a fairly standard schedule for distance runners in
the late 1950s in the States. It's no wonder that Buddy hit a plateau
in college.

"In changing his program to give it some muscle, I talked a
lot to Buddy about the need to adapt gradually to increased stress.
We called it GAS, which is short for '
and analogized it to the legend of M
birth to its death as a means of assur
tance. That's what we wanted in Bu
to overload him up front.

"Buddy had a leg infectio
year at Minnesota and never got goin
The year was more transition than
right. Even then we were thinking

the 10,000 meters. We had our eyes on the U.S. team for the Rome Olympics in 1960.

"Buddy finished his eligibility at the University in the spring of 1959 and our serious preparation began. I had a friend in Finland and we sent Buddy over there that summer to live with him and race. I don't recall that he raced particularly well but at least it opened his eyes. The Europeans were playing a different game; they were accepting sacrifices that most of our guys didn't even consider. Buddy also spent some time that summer with Pat Clohessy, one of the Australians who was running at the University of Houston at the time. Pat was a student of the distance events and no doubt a favorable influence on Buddy.

"Buddy came back to the University of Minnesota in 1959 to finish his degree. During that fall and into the next semester, he continued to bring the volume of his training to an appropriate level. By the spring of 1960, as we pointed to the Olympic trials in California, Buddy was doing workouts like 25 x 440 in 68 seconds each, with a minute jog. Or he might do 4 x 2 miles with four minute intervals. He was putting in almost 18 miles a day, broken into two separate sessions.

"He responded very well to the increased effort. That winter, for example, he went to the Massachusetts Knights of Columbus Indoor Meet and won the invitational three mile in good time, 13:58, over Deacon Jones among others, and did it straight from the front. At that race he went through two miles in 9:14 which, a year or two earlier, would have been all he could do for the distance, never mind adding an extra mile to it. Later in the spring, he doubled at the Mt. San Antonio College Relays, running 5,000 meters in 14:48.7 and 10,000 meters in 30:35. He also won the Drake Relays' 5,000-meter run in 14:35.7 and finished second to Al ____ence of Australia in the Coliseum Relays' 5,000-meter run in ____ In early May, he ran a 10K at an all-comers meet in ____ California, with the expressed intention of breaking ____ American record, which was 30:19. In a race which ended almost at midnight and with only about a hundred people in the stands to watch it, Buddy ran splits of 4:48 for the one mile, 9:41 for two, 14:33 for the three miles, four miles in 19:21, five in 24:13, six miles in 29:01 and finished with a last quarter in 66.2, for a final time of 29:58.9, an American record and the first time an American had been under 30 minutes for the event. Admittedly, this says something about the state of American distance running in that the Olympic qualifying time was 29:40, but it still shows progress. Buddy felt afterwards that it was the easiest race he had ever run and was confident that if Al Lawrence or someone of that caliber had been in the race to help with the pace, he could have run 29:30.

"Unfortunately, the day of the 10,000-meters Olympic Trial was hot and Buddy did not run well. The officials used the AAU meet as the qualifier, which was a distinct meet from the Final Trials in which the other members of the Olympic team would be chosen, and the AAU meet got a long way behind schedule. The 10,000 meters didn't start until a minute or two before midnight. But the real problem was that Buddy was anemic. Even at that, he stayed with the pace until the four-mile mark, running with Al Lawrence; Doug Lyle, a Canadian; Max Truex, who later smashed the American record for 10,000 meters in finishing sixth at Rome; Billy Mills and Mal Robertson. But Buddy let go shortly after that and eventually drifted to tenth place in 31:26.9. Truex picked up the place on the Olympic team by running a time well within Buddy's normal range, 30:16.3, but what comfort was there in that? We had a blood test right after the race and found that Buddy's hemoglobin count was down to 12.5 grams per 100cc. The explanation was obvious. Buddy had a tendency to put on weight unless he was careful. On this occasion, his care went a bit far and he was undernourished. No matter how carefully you train, you can't run unless you take note of the basics first: get the rest and the food you need. Anyway, Buddy just shattered that day and we were both a little disappointed. But that happens and we weren't finished. The first thing we tried was to qualify Buddy for the Olympic Trials' 5,000 meters, but Buddy was so seriously underpar at the AAU meet that he could not even get up to seventh place in the event, the last qualifying spot. His time for 5,000 meters was 14:50. Ironically, Lew Stieglitz took the last spot, and he was the person who held the American record over 10,000 meters before Buddy broke it earlier in the spring.

"We still had one chance to get Buddy into the 1960 Olympics. In the 10,000 meters, two spots were still open because no Americans had met the Olympic qualifying standard for the event. If Buddy could do that he might still join Truex on the team for Rome. But we couldn't find a race here in the United States so we sent him to Finland again, hoping he could get into a competitive race and qualify. We didn't know then, of course, that he wouldn't return to live in the United States for more than five years.

"As it happened, the trip to Finland was something of a hardship. Buddy was supposed to work on board to pay his way, chipping paint off the deck or some such thing, which must have been fine because the boat was so small that it only had about 30 yards' worth of deck. But the trip took several weeks, as I recall, and by the time Buddy got to Finland he was in no shape to run to an Olympic qualifying standard. Nonetheless, he set to work on it. He stayed again with this friend of mine, trained and raced. We had one problem though. The only race scheduled at 10,000 meters was the Finnish national championships, and they did not permit foreigners to run it. So Buddy did not get a chance to run an Olympic qualifying time and did not make the United States Olympic team in 1960.

"But at least he started to train well. He was running on different terrains, one day on the track, the next on grass and the next on the road. He was blending interval work, good running like 30 x 400 meters in 72-73 with 200-meter jog between each or 5 x 2 miles in 10:40 each with four minutes between them. He'd do 30-40 x 100 meters. Other days, it was fartlek, sometimes getting 20 miles of it. And of course he had the usual complement of long runs on the road, although nothing as long as he would do later.

"This was a strange interlude actually. Buddy was there in

Finland, eventually teaching English to people who answered an ad he put in the paper, and he was running regularly, competing as he could but with nothing definite on the horizon. Meanwhile at the Olympics in Rome, Bikila was revolutionizing the marathon."

CHAPTER THREE

*Will he not fancy that the shadows
which he formerly saw are truer
than the objects which are now shown to him?*

Dialogues of Plato, The Republic, VII

Abebe Bikila moved lightly through stages of his own imagining: forbearance, indifference, disdain. He was a figure of rumor in 1960, reported to have run an extraordinary time at altitude over the full marathon distance but with nothing more to sustain him—to all appearances another of the legion of African runners meant for quick front-running bursts followed by heartrending sometimes comical recession back to the pack and beyond. Like the other African runners with him in Rome for the Olympic Games, he was a shadow on the wall, evocative and suggestive, but nothing for immediate concern.

In the event, Bikila ran barefoot in Rome with Rhadi, two Africans to a beat of their own, far ahead of Keily, Popov, Vandendriessche, Magee and Saoudi. The two worked together to 40 kilometers up a slight rise headed for the Obelisk of Axum and then Bikila accelerated in the darkness of artificial light to the Arch of Constantine and a startling, impassive victory.

Bikila. After Rome the name meant concentration and it meant nature and it meant solitude and it meant mystery. The man Bikila was Africa, and Africa was unknown.

Every world-class marathoner in the early 1960s trained daily with Bikila while Bikila trained alone in Ethiopia. To those unseen training with him, he ran easily, as gently as he appeared on race day, unfairly assisted by his environment, by his proximity to it, by nature itself with which he was one. As with many other successful black athletes, his victories were credited to God or something akin, to "natural ability," to the wind and to the mountains, but never to the hard work of which only whites were capable and to which only they would submit.

Without denying Bikila's talents or the advantage of birth and life at altitude, everything else which explained his preeminence was legend or racism or fear or regret. A brief glimpse of Bikila's training is enough to establish that it was hard work and well conceived. In the last 11 days before his departure for Rome, for example, Bikila did his training at an altitude of 5,900 feet, as follows:

June 27 - (morning) one hour of varying work over the hills: 300 meters of climbing followed by 300 meters of easy running, repeatedly. (afternoon) 4 x 1,500 meters on the track in times varying between 4:12 and 4:18 at five-minute intervals, then a sauna. Bikila warmed up for each session with 20 minutes of easy running.

June 28 - 32 kilometers on road without shoes in 1:45.

June 29 - rest.

June 30 - 32 kilometers on the road with shoes in 1:46:30.

July 1 - (morning) 5 x 1,500 meters on the track at five-minute intervals, successively in 4:12, 4:18, 4:13, 4:14 and 4:14. (afternoon) 45 minutes of running on varied terrain.

July 2 - series of fast, straight runs on the track interspersed with jogs around the turns; duration of 45 minutes.

July 3 - rest.

July 4 - (morning) 1 1/2 hours running on varied ground. (afternoon) 3 x 1,500 meters in 4:13, 4:15 and 4:15.

Emil Zatopek ran 2:23:03 at Helsinki. Alain Mimoun ran 2:25:00 to win the 1956 Olympic Marathon at Melbourne. Abebe Bikila ran 2:15:16 at Rome.

Zatopek and Peters, and later the Soviet Union's Popov in the European Championships of 1958, used speed to increase the pace at which each of the 26 miles of the marathon could be comfortably run. Bikila not only ran faster over the body of the marathon, which was itself an effective use of speed, he used his speed tactically, by picking a moment at 40 kilometers and moving. In so doing, he changed the marathon from run to race. After Bikila the marathon was not substantively different from the shorter track distances. Speed, and how it was used, together with strength and endurance, determined the result. Attrition, once the definition of this event, was now a mere incident of it.

CHAPTER FOUR

"I became a distance runner the moment
I stepped foot in England."

By November 1960, Buddy Edelen was ready to leave Finland. The Olympic Games, which had initially drawn him to the country, were concluded. Beyond that, Finland's tradition of successful distance running, which might once have prompted Buddy to stay, was still and quiet, like the statue of Paavo Nurmi frozen outside the Helsinki stadium. So on November 11 Buddy boarded the Russian passenger ship, the Latvia. His destination was England.

Buddy shared the ship with its Russian crew and, thankfully, with a number of attractive Finnish women. The women were an aesthetic success, but it was Buddy's interaction with the crew that had a more enduring impact. The crew and Buddy gathered one evening to watch a film of the first dual meet between track and field teams from the United States and the Soviet Union, which had been held in the summer of 1958 in Moscow. The United States won the meet 126 to 109 but the Russians were amused by Buddy's event, the 10,000 meters, a strength for the Soviet Union from the time Kuts arrived in 1954 and continuing through the date of this meet. The Soviets entered Zhukov and Desyathikov. The Americans countered with McKenzie and Smartt.

Buddy knew Jerry Smartt. Jerry ran for the University of Houston when Buddy was at Minnesota. In the cross-country season of 1958, in fact, Buddy finished one place behind Jerry at the national collegiate championships. Jerry was a small, thin man blessed with subtle talent, but he was a personable member of America's long-distance community and Buddy liked him. Buddy watched with interest, then, in this dual meet as the two Soviets established immediate control and ran essentially uncontested. He watched McKenzie trail badly, step completely off the track and then step back on, apparently with a change of heart, only to be disqualified. And he watched his friend Jerry lose contact and finish nearly a minute behind even the second Russian runner, never mind the first.

Admittedly Jerry's run was not a good one, but it shook Buddy to hear the crew laugh at Jerry's performance. That laughter was personally offensive to him. More generally, it was an insult to America and its capacity as a society, or incapacity as the Russians would have it, to produce men capable of dominating the long run. Buddy stored the memory of that laughter. On difficult days, when snow or rain fell, when an injury nagged and tempted him to back off, when a competitor applied the pace and it hurt, he took this one memory off the shelf.

. .

Buddy arrived in England on November 16, 1960. He intended to find a teaching job and stay awhile. His contact was Derek Cole, a businessman in the London area and a friendly acquaintance of Fred's. Buddy stayed with Derek until he found employment as a teacher at the King John Modern Secondary School in early 1961 and got his own place. In the meantime and for some time thereafter, he ran for Derek's athletics club, Chelmsford.

CHAPTER FIVE

"I fell twice but so did everyone else."

The English take a proprietary interest in cross-country. For some reason, they appreciate and claim as their own an ability to run over plowed fields, through and into streams, in deep mud and muck, over fences and walls. So close is the identification between uncomfortable conditions and cross-country that an Englishman who runs badly will almost certainly say that the course was too dry or too flat, thereby altogether wrong and not, in fact, the genuine article.

Having arrived in England on the 16th, Buddy contested his first cross-country meet for Chelmsford three days later, on the 19th. He was fit enough, having lost only a few days on the Latvia, and he was a former Big Ten cross-country champion so he did not expect to be outclassed. On the other hand, the English took rather a different view. A Yank in cross-country would be off the golf course and into the open field for the first time; that, they thought, should spell an absolutely fascinating disaster. Buddy knew what was expected of him and made himself a silent promise: it would be hard on everyone.

The course was five miles and reputed to be among the most difficult in all the country, full of hills, uneven footing and boggy mud. The weather was wet. Buddy did not jog the course in advance; he delivered himself into it at the gun and hoped for the best, driving hard all the way from the front. The headline in the next day's paper said it all: AMERICAN TAKE-OVER IN CROSS-COUNTRY. The account recorded with surprise that Edelen led from the start, managed the course in good fashion and won handily in the Southeast Essex cross-country league match over his teammate and occasional British international athlete Brian Hill-Cottingham.

The time was inconsequential. What was significant was that Buddy led and that he appeared to enjoy himself. In his diary, Buddy left no doubt about the matter:

"This was a race over a course I will never forget! The course was five miles of continuous mud. A really true c.c. course over hill, fences, plowed field. I fell twice but so did every one else, I think, due to the knee deep mud and slop of which most of the course consisted. I enjoyed this race much more than any I have run before. It is truly cross-country!"

The first cross-country meet was followed by the first road relay and in turn by road races and track meets, all for the sake of the club, and for the purpose of moving Buddy gradually up in competitive distance, while keeping him sharp enough to run such distances fast.

· ·

The year that opened as Buddy entered England and began competing for Chelmsford, 1961, was a dead year in international athletics. The calendar offered no Olympics, no Commonwealth Games, no European championships. It was a year in which the races were only building blocks for the next year. Buddy raced in that manner throughout 1961.

On January 29, 1961, Buddy became the first American to compete in a major European cross-country event. The race was in San Sebastian, Spain, and attracted some of Europe's top performers. Buddy's running was described as brilliant in the newspaper reports, although he finished only seventh. The description of the run as

Buddy follows Basil Heatley over a cross-country hurdle.

brilliant was, no doubt, a reflection of the reporter's surprise that an American was there at all, and somewhat less an acknowledgement that he beat several of England's top runners, including Alan Perkins and Mike Wiggs, in the process.

Buddy also finished seventh on February 5 over seven miles at the Hannut, Belgium, cross-country meet, finishing behind Rhadi and Gaston Roelants among others. A measure of his consistency, if not his improvement, was the fact that he beat three of the runners who had finished in front of him in San Sebastian. Basil Heatley of England, the winner of the national cross-country meet in Britain in 1960 and destined to repeat this year, outkicked him for sixth but was the only Englishman in front of him.

Based on the results in Europe, Buddy hoped to run well at one of England's most prestigious cross-country meets, the Southern County cross-country championships. On February 18, he finished fourth in the meeting, ahead of such respected English runners as Mike Wiggs, Bruce Tulloh, Stan Eldon and Gordon Pirie. Over the nine-mile course Buddy was second to Martin Hyman until the last 100 yards when he just could not hold off Jim Hogan of Ireland and Alan Perkins.

Buddy subsequently moved up in distance and onto the road. He won a half marathon in 1:04:37 before adding a win in the Finchley Twenty Miler in 1:45:30. He then ran three miles in 13:54 and followed it with a 3,000 meters in Warsaw in 8:17, moving up and down in distance to develop strength and speed.

The goal race for the summer of 1961 was the Amateur Athletic Association six-mile championship held on July 14. Buddy was fit and rested and he should have run well. He was, however, a disappointed eighth in 28:59, having never been a factor. Dave Power of Australia won ahead of Heatley. The problem was one of will. As the leading group of six accelerated after two miles, Buddy did not. As a result, he spent the rest of the race leading a second pack, working just as hard as the people up front but with no reasonable expectation of reward. Fred Wilt had warned him that in every race there is a moment when the athlete must commit himself; if he fails, he is lost. On this occasion the moment came and went.

Buddy knew the fault was his, which made things all the worse. This run should have been a step forward. Instead it was nothing. Buddy finished disgusted with himself for having lost contact. "I rested plenty before the race and thought I'd run a blinder, but I didn't." Fred responded to the AAA result philosophically, reminding Buddy not to grow discouraged. "We all make mistakes," Fred wrote, "and you will probably never again let them break contact with you. The 28:59 was most respectable."

With that, Buddy picked up the thread of his racing and training. On September 23, he won the Bernie Hames Half Marathon in 1:07:43 after losing his shoe to an untied lace at the six-mile marker and running the last seven miles barefoot. Although his feet were cut and his time was slow, Buddy was satisfied to win by a minute, under the circumstances.

.   .   .

In contrast to the racing, which was merely good, Buddy's training was much improved. It combined volume and quality as never before. The training was consistent from week to week. The period from Sunday, October 29, through Sunday, November 5, 1961, is typical:

Sunday: 21 miles from Chelmsford to Southend in 1:55. This was a moderate run. Buddy ran with a high school and Minnesota team member, Bill Erickson. Bill was a former Big Ten champion over 1,000 yards indoors and was in England for the year. Because Bill was not in his best condition, Buddy ran hard for several miles, went back for Bill, ran hard again, went back and then ran hard, continuing throughout.

Monday: a.m. 2 x 2 miles in 10:15 and 10:25 with 3-min. jog interval; then 25 x 100 yards with 30-yard jog interval.
p.m. 4 x 1 mile in 4:55; 4:52; 4:41; and 4:53 with 3-min. jog.

Tuesday: a.m. one-mile jog to sea front; followed by 2 x 2 mile; 9:41 and 10:26.
p.m. rest.

Wednesday: a.m. one-mile run to sea front; 30 x 440 avg. 68 with 60-second jog interval.
p.m. 3/4 mile warm-up; 2 x steady run; 25 x 120 yards.

Thursday: 9 miles.

In full flight, against former mile world-record holder and Olympic
Bronze Medalist Derek Ibbotson.

Friday: One-mile warm-up; 4 x 1 mile in 4:52; 4:43; 5:07 and 5:06 with three-minute jog interval; one-mile warm-down.

Saturday: 4-mile cross-country race in 17:25 (time as given). First, over Mel Batty. "I ran like a bomb today."

Sunday: 21 miles in 1:53.

Generally, the continued focus of Buddy's training was interval-oriented, but the volume of that work was increasing as was the quality. The long run at or near race pace on Sunday was becoming regular, but by no means inevitable.

. . . .

In all of 1961 the most significant race for Buddy may have been the one he didn't run. The United States had agreed to meet the United Kingdom in a dual meet. The meet was scheduled in the White City Stadium on July 22. Buddy wanted to be on the U.S. team. He was a former American record holder over 10,000 meters, he was running well and he only lived a relatively few miles down the road from the venue.

In the ordinary course the AAU, America's governing body in amateur athletics, selected its team members from among the participants in the national meet, which was, of course, held in the United States. The method of selection presumed that all of America's best athletes would be at the AAU meet. It did not take into account a person living outside the country and unable to attend the AAU meet because of expense. Buddy hoped therefore that the AAU would make an exception for him and let him run. It was a faint hope indeed and it did not happen.

On July 22, Buddy was not on the track; he was in the stands. He watched as the two American runners in the six-mile run were lapped, the nearest of them finishing two minutes behind the second

Briton. And he heard once more the laughter around him. It was another reminder of the low reputation of American distance running and of how well earned that reputation was. But this time it was also a lesson. Buddy would never be able to afford a trip to the AAU meet to run a qualifier there. In that case, he had to force an exception if he wanted on the national team. The only way to do that was to run so fast that they must notice him.

In the meantime, Buddy decided that a gesture would be in order. For some time thereafter, he ran his races not in the vest of the United States, which he would have preferred, but in a plain shirt marked only by a stark "W." Wilt.

Fred himself covered the entire situation with one remark: "Those bums!"

Through it all, Buddy continued his training, during the late summer and fall of 1961, looking forward to the next cross-country season.

CHAPTER SIX

*"I worked my way up and soon
Roelants and I were carving it up."*

It was three years before Gaston Roelants would win an Olympic Gold Medal but he was already a national hero in Belgium on Christmas Day 1961. Buddy went to Louvain on that day to race him in his home town. The course was eight laps in the town park for a total distance of eight kilometers.

It was a small affair; nevertheless it was Buddy's entry to international success. The flavor of the race was captured in local reports of the running, variously titled "Surprise at the Louvain cross-country running," "Surprise at Louvain where Gaston Roelants is comfortably beaten by the American Edelen," and "Een Amerikaans veldloper, Buddy Edelen, verslaat Gaston Roelants voor eigen volk te Leuven."

One report analyzed the disappointing result in the following terms:

"On Monday, too, Roelants made the mistake of attacking too soon. During the first four laps—the course consisted of eight—he took the offensive at each climb of the steep bank which marked the arrival line. His stamina inevitably broke."

Shadowing future Olympic Gold Medalist Gaston Roelants of Belgium.

Another report was more inclined to note Buddy's participation in the event, rather than reproach Roelants for his boldness:

"*On the frozen ground of the Louvain Park, with its numerous banks and its two climbs which are so hard on the legs, Roelants tried several times to shake off the American. Already little Gaston's face was perspiring, a factor which is rarely a good sign with him in the course of a race, whilst Edelen seemed to be untroubled by the Belgian's successive spurts, especially on the climbs. The two men forged on together for two more kilometers. Then the unexpected happened.*

"*After a new and unsuccessful attack by Roelants, Buddy Edelen threw off his gloves, a gesture which was to prove deadly because it was decisive. Gaston Roelants was never able to overtake the American after that—on the contrary, he only lost ground to his rival. The latter maintained his effort splendidly, running with great ease and making a fine impression. The public, very sportingly, warmly applauded him for his achievement.*"

44

Always a popular guest, Buddy celebrates with his host family in Louvain.

     Buddy recollects the event with similar surprise. As he tells it, he followed Roelants expecting momentarily to be left in the wake. When it did not happen, he went by Gaston, gave him a little pat and ran like the dickens, hoping he could make it a hundred yards. A hundred yards later he decided to run hard for another hundred yards. A hundred yards later and he was alone.

     However, a runner cannot truly be beaten in his home town, even if he happens to run badly. On this day, the race promoters, satisfied that Gaston would win as he always did, had asked him what he wanted as his first prize. Gaston said he wanted a divan and picked out a big, heavy thing. When Buddy won, he was offered the divan but could not transport it back to his flat, which could not have accommodated it anyway. So the divan went to Gaston after all and Buddy got the second prize, an electric razor.

     December 1961 was not likely to find Gaston Roelants in his best form, and Buddy did not draw too broad a conclusion from the outcome of the race in Louvain. Roelants was a flier and especially at a distance as short as eight kilometers, beating him again was unlikely. That fact notwithstanding, Buddy recognized from the victory that he had drawn level with the best in Europe. He might not beat them but he would be competitive. For an American in the early 1960s, that was extraordinary.

CHAPTER SEVEN

74, 74, 71, 71, 73, 72, 73, 72, 74, 72, 73, 73,
73, 74, 73, 73, 72, 73, 73, 74, 73, 75, 74, 73,
71, 73, 73, 73, 75, 74, 76, 73, 72, 74, 75, 75,
69, 70, 70, 66.8

Entering 1962, Buddy was a marathoner in search of the right moment. His mileage was well over 100 miles a week, most of it fast, and it included a weekly long run, which he gradually increased over the winter and early spring to a full 26 miles. Buddy had in mind the marathon of the Polytechnic Harriers, scheduled in June. Between the year's start and the Poly, however, lay a thousand and more miles of training and a number of important races, each one of which could profit from and be part of the marathon work which surrounded it.

The first important race was the Southern cross-country championships at Reading. The course was three laps of three miles and it was dry. Starting slowly, Buddy worked his way to sixth after one lap, sharing the effort with Jim Hogan, Bruce Tulloh, Mel Batty, Martin Hyman, Alan Perkins and Brian Hill-Cottingham. Unfortunately, he felt terrible. On the second lap, he was pleased to see that Hogan felt even worse. Hogan fell back and then the others in turn, so Buddy kept at it. Batty remained. Buddy had been training with Mel of late and he knew that 100 yards down at eight miles this race was lost. On instinct, he gave it one more push and was satisfied to see the margin close. Mel, however, reacted in an unfriendly manner. He

Mel Batty carries the pace while Buddy waits his turn.

sprinted. Buddy finished second.

It would have been better to win but the effort was gratifying. Buddy was particularly pleased to note how uncomfortable his hosts had been at the prospect of an American victory and how measurable the relief was when he lost. One account headlined: THE ELEC-TRICIAN STOPS A SHOCK, before reporting that "Melvin Batty, a Thurrock (Essex) electrician, saved the face of British athletics on Saturday. He prevented an AMERICAN winning the Southern Counties cross-country championship at Reading from more than 500 British runners."

Backhanded or no, the article was inherently complimentary and Buddy knew it. He redoubled his efforts with the intention of creating a greater stir down the line. The next opportunity was at the Amateur Athletics Association (AAA) 10-mile British national championships on April 21, on the cinder track at Hurlingham. It was the first important track event of the season.

Nine runners went to the line in dull, breezy conditions. Of the nine, Mel Batty and Gerry North presented the greatest difficulty and, from the start, these two carried the pace. For once, Buddy did no more than his fair share of the work, and maybe even a little less. North led, Batty ran wide at the curb and Buddy followed. The three stayed this way through six-miles at 29:12. Buddy expected to feel this pace, given that his best over the six-mile distance was only 28:54, but he felt fine. He settled where he was and watched without concern as Mel moved up and through 10,000 meters in 30:10.

Buddy figured that in this company he had the best speed. But he might be wrong, after all, so he decided on a sure, swift move deep enough into the race that everyone would be tired but close enough to home that speed would count. In the meantime, he tucked behind Mel and Gerry through seven miles in 34:01.8, through eight miles in 38:59.2 and through nine in 43:55.6, American records at each intermediate distance. Nine was the time. Buddy went to the lead and added a 69-second lap to the 36 quarter miles which had preceded it. Gerry and Mel hung for a stride or two and were gone. 70, 70, 66.8 and it was over.

The first American since 1887 to win an AAA distance crown.

Buddy's winning time was 48:31.8. Buddy was now the fourth fastest 10-miler in history, behind only Basil Heatley, Zatopek and Rhadi. He had the additional satisfaction of beating the American record by a full 2 minutes and 18 seconds.

"The Killer Yank zips to Treble Triumph," said one paper, while the next reported more sedately a surprising "Buddy blow to Britain's athletes." Buddy was the first American to win an AAA distance event since one E. C. Carter won the four mile and the 10-mile in 1887. Hearing an account of the race, Fred reminded Buddy that the AAA 10-mile championship was "a feat to remember but this is only the start."

CHAPTER EIGHT

"Are you a betting man?"

"Buddy Edelen, an American residing in England for the specific purpose of bettering his performance in long-distance races," wrote Frank Downey, "is an attractive visitor to the John F. Kennedy Stadium, Santry, on Sunday (11:30) where in the one-hour run he hopes to achieve one of his ambitions by beating Emil Zatopek's world record for the event."

Buddy, at the invitation of Irish promoter Billy Morton, was in Ireland with Brian Kilby and Gerry North for the run. Buddy had his usual deal. If Billy would pay expenses, Buddy would run. The trip to Ireland was bonus enough. On the other hand, Billy Morton was an athlete's promoter. Even if you did not have your hand out, he would put something in it. Shortly before this one-hour run, Billy with a friend visited Buddy in his room. After the greeting, Billy got to the point. "Buddy, me lad," he said, "are ya a betting man?" Buddy said he was, so Billy explained the way things were.

"Buddy," he said, "I can't pay you anything for this race because you're an amateur. But seein' as how you're a betting man," and he paused for effect before pointing to Buddy's suitcase on the floor, "I bet you a hundred quid you can't jump over that suitcase."

As the meaning of Billy's wager struck home, Buddy quickly hopped over the suitcase. Morton exclaimed loudly at such a thing, "My God, Tommy, look at that, Buddy just took me for a 100 quid!" but being a man of his word, he paid the money and left. Buddy was 100 quid richer, but he was still an amateur.

· ·

The one-hour run was held on a Sunday morning at Santry Stadium before a packed crowd of about five people. The morning was humid and the several runners worked hard against a standard they would not meet. North, Kilby and Edelen shared the work through a 4:46 mile, a 9:36 two mile, three in 14:26 and six in 29:12. Thereafter Buddy drifted a little, getting as far as 35 yards behind before regaining contact at the 49:22 10-mile split. He even led at 11. But the next half mile did him in, and Kilby went off, finally running 12 miles and 178 yards in the hour. Buddy was second with 12 miles and 151 yards. Gerry North covered 12 miles and 115 yards.

Although he, and everyone else, failed to break Zatopek's world record, Buddy at least had the satisfaction of beating Pete McArdle's American record. And, of course, a hard hour on the track was excellent preparation for his first marathon.

CHAPTER NINE

"This was a nightmare for me!"

Disappointed by the poor showing of British athletes in the 1908 Olympic Marathon, *The Sporting Life Magazine* offered in 1909 a 500-pound silver trophy to the winner of an annually held road race of not less than 25 miles. The Polytechnic Harriers accepted the obligation of sponsoring such an event and thereby began the first and for many years the pre-eminent marathon in the United Kingdom. The best marathoners in England ran the Poly. Sam Ferris, Tom Richards and Jack Holden each finished first more than once. Jim Peters won four years in a row between 1951 and 1954, leaving the event record at 2:17:39.

Although the course changed from time to time, the traditional Polytechnic Marathon ran from Windsor Castle along the Thames River to the stadium in Chiswick. It was flat to gently downhill, with no significant hills to worry a runner. The Poly was fast.

• •

Buddy entered the Polytechnic Marathon to be held on June 16, 1962. It was his first marathon and he was ready. In the final week of training, he put what he considered a little snap in it, using the Tuesday before the Saturday event to run 45 x 110 and Wednesday to run 20 x 440 at 70.5. The next day, Thursday, he jogged easily and on Friday he rested.

·   ·   ·

Shortly before 3 o'clock on race day, the 200 marathoners left the changing rooms and were admitted into the grounds of the castle proper. The runners lined in two rows along "The Long Walk," which stretched three miles to the Great Park and the Copper Horse. With all in readiness, the Queen of England arrived to start the race. As she walked through the runners she stopped occasionally for small talk, including a moment with Buddy. He said about what you would expect a young man from Sioux Falls, South Dakota, to say to the Queen of England moments before beginning the marathon for which he had trained years. "Hi, Queen!"

Buddy meets the Queen before his first marathon.
Notice the similarity in headgear.

At 3:15 in warm, sunny weather the Queen started the runners on the way to Chiswick. Immediately Buddy was in trouble. On the morning of the race Buddy had been offered and had accepted a can of sardines for breakfast from his best friend, Bill Erickson. In the ordinary course, he might have turned the sardines down and had toast and eggs, for instance, perhaps with a cup of coffee or juice.

That apparently reasonable option overlooks the mind games athletes play. They manipulate events. For example, when a good runner does something prudent in preparation for a race, he expects to run well because he has been prudent. On the other hand, from time to time, a good athlete feels the burden of expectations and does something imprudent, stupid if you will, intentionally. The athlete knows that if he does this stupid thing he will run well because doing a stupid thing, a self-destructive thing, relieves the pressure on the athlete by giving him an excuse to fail. With that excuse in place, he can relax. Relaxed he will run well. It is an athlete's version of Catch-22. No matter whether he is prudent or imprudent he will run well. So Buddy ate the can of sardines on the morning of his first marathon.

By six miles Buddy was catching sardines on the way up; in so doing he became nauseous and cramped; nauseous and cramped, his legs went out from underneath him. As his legs went out, he slowed; as he slowed, he grew discouraged; as he grew discouraged, he slowed. Buddy trudged along the road from Windsor Castle to Chiswick Stadium without any hope in the world. Up in front a race was being run and he had no place in it.

At least one athletics expert had picked Buddy to win this race, saying boldly that "the Polytechnic Harriers race Windsor to Chiswick, which is to be started by the Queen today, should be won by a runner who has never run more than 20 miles before." That was Buddy. The writer felt, quite rightly in the ordinary case, that Buddy would have the great advantage of speed. In support of that proposition, the writer referred to a recent performance over 3,000 meters, in which Buddy ran 8:10.

Unfortunately, Buddy used no speed in his inaugural marathon. He used only his determination to finish what he started, no matter how forlornly. At the end, Ron Hill, running the second of many marathons in his storied career, won easily in 2:21:59. Buddy got home in 2:31 for ninth, wondering where the promise of spring went.

· · · ·

Fred Wilt advised Buddy in his training and, by and large, Buddy acquiesced. Particularly if Fred suggested the need to run more or faster, Buddy embraced the notion and went to it. However, Fred often advised that the long, hard running should be broken by periods of complete rest. Within 10 days of the Poly in 1962, Fred found at least three times that Buddy ran when he should have rested. On June 8 Buddy ran 25 minutes, an inoffensive workout on its face but one which brought Fred up: "This is OK and didn't hurt you, but I would rather see you have the complete courage and faith in yourself to take a day or two of complete rest. It is so very good for the mind!!!" The next day Buddy did 30 minutes and again Fred would have preferred rest: "Again, this cannot harm you but if there is anything to be gained it is from COMPLETE rest. I do wish you could develop the self-confidence to TRUST yourself. I have far more confidence in Edelen than you have." Finally, on the Thursday before the Poly, Buddy ran 40 minutes and Fred wrote: "I can't say this 40-minute jog hurt you. I can say it does not help two days before a race. This is a manifestation of uncertainty. There is a time to train and a time to rest—not halfway rest. This is a bitter lesson you have not accepted." Of course, Fred Wilt's comments came after the bad run at the Poly, because his reviews lagged until Buddy mailed the diary sheets to him. Nonetheless, these remarks were typical of a continuing battle between adviser and athlete and of undoubted value in explaining what happened at the Poly.

Along this line, the two hard workouts within five days of the marathon surely also must be considered. 45 x 110 on the Tuesday and 20 x 440 on the Wednesday may have been excessive and contributed to the dead legs Buddy carried under him in his first marathon. Buddy's diet was also part of the problem. By the early 1960s, only a relative few marathoners, Clarence DeMar among them, had recognized the value of carbohydrates as a pre-race staple. Buddy did not, and his diet in the days before the Poly was light, in order to control his weight, and included no carbohydrates even incidentally.

Finally, the sardines. Sometimes, as it happens, a self-destructive act is in fact self-destructive and it doesn't make a bit of difference whether the athlete is relaxed or not. He can't run.

· · · · ·

"This was a nightmare for me! I ran very badly. I felt tired from six miles, mainly in the legs. I started moderately slow, but felt my legs get sore and tired at six miles. I was about 50 seconds down on the leaders at five miles, but then closed before losing again. I then went slower and slower. Last 15 miles were sheer hell, and every step my legs felt as if they were going to give out on me. I felt good in the upper body—breathing easy, but it was my legs and my guts. I don't think I averaged seven minute miles the last six! Never came so close to quitting a race before. I never want to run a race when I feel like that again!"

CHAPTER TEN

"I was really hurting the last four miles,
but nothing as bad as the Poly."

Immediately after the Poly, Buddy was finished with marathoning. He wasn't going to do that again. Whatever success he had over shorter distances, even distances up to 20 miles, had nothing to do with the marathon and he was no marathoner. That lasted a moment, maybe longer, but certainly no longer than the time it took Buddy's headmaster, Bert Evans, to talk with him about the Welsh Marathon Championships scheduled on July 21. In fairness, Buddy thought he should have another go at it. If this one blew up in his face, that would do it, definitely, no kidding, never again, that's the last time, I mean it.

Between the bad Poly and Wales, Buddy spent a few days in Prague. On June 23, he ran 5,000 meters in 14:14, good running only seven days after the marathon. He then ran modestly, even adding a couple of days of total rest, before contesting the AAA six-mile championships in the White City Stadium.

The AAA was too fast for Buddy. He hoped to run 24 70-second quarters for a final time of 28:00. He did well through two miles in 9:18 and three in 14:01 but he lost the main pack of six or seven there. He ran alone for the next two miles, ahead of Ron Hill and Brian

Kilby among others, before finding the energy to run a hard final mile, passing Alan Perkins in the last 100 yards and closing on Basil Heatley, who held only three seconds on him when they stopped.

As it turned out, Buddy would have lost this race even if he maintained goal pace. Roy Fowler won the race in a dead heat from Mike Bullivant, with both in 27:49. Buddy finished eighth in 28:26. His time was an American record, which was fine, but that only emphasized the extent to which Americans lagged in this event—an American record behind seven Britons!

. .

Jim Peters set the Welsh all-comers marathon record in 1953 at 2:22:29. Tom Richards held the championship record at 2:30:40 and had for 10 years. Neither record gave Buddy a moment's pause as he contemplated the event. He just needed to finish in some orderly fashion, to hold together and find out whether this event could be managed or not.

In the eight days before the Saturday start he had four days of either complete rest or easy jogging, interrupted by a set of 40 quarters in 73-74 on Tuesday afternoon and 2 x 2 miles in 9:54 and 9:57 on Wednesday. He did not run on Thursday, and on Friday he merely jogged 15 to 20 minutes to loosen up after a seven-hour drive to Wales.

Buddy ate more than he did before the Poly. This was consistent with Fred's new theory that a marathoner should carry one to three extra pounds into the event to tide him over for the demands of 26 miles of running. In the last few days before this marathon, Buddy indulged himself with cakes and pastry in addition to the ordinary meals. He ate no sardines.

. . .

The course was out and back and the day was windy, blowing strongly at the back of the runners on the way out and into them on the return. Buddy stayed with a pack of seven runners until the five-mile mark in 29:41. He then moved away with John Tarrant through 10 miles before accelerating on a long grade approaching Castleton. By 15 miles, he was on his own. He ducked his head down against his chest, kept running, cursed the wind and just tried to get the thing done. He felt he was hardly moving the last three miles, but he took one step at a time until at last it was over.

Buddy's time of 2:22:33 just missed Jim Peters' all-comers mark by four seconds but it destroyed Tom Richards' event record by 10 minutes. John Tarrant, after a misdirection in the parking lot outside the stadium and after a cramp that almost stopped him, finished more than a mile behind Buddy in a time of 2:31:41.

The Welsh Marathon turned Buddy around. Poly was the aberration.

. . . .

"I'm really pleased with this! The wind was terribly strong with gusts over 40 mph the last 12 miles. It was really tough. We started slowly (six-minute pace). At five miles, John Tarrant broke away up a long steep hill and I went with him. I felt good. The pace was steady until eight miles when I tried to break away up a hill. He caught me at the top again. Then at 10 miles, I really pushed it and he faded. Once he went, I really piled it on. I felt very good until we hit the wind coming back. I still pushed it all the way and did, in fact, feel good until 17 miles when I started to tire rapidly. I was really hurting the last four miles, but nothing as bad as the Poly."

CHAPTER ELEVEN

"No one would lead."

Shortly after the victory in Wales, Buddy left the Chelmsford Athletic Club to join Hadleigh Olympiad, closer to his school. Later that summer he received his first invitation to compete in an international marathon, Kosice. The International Peace Marathon in Kosice, Czechoslovakia, was conceived by a group of Czech officials in attendance at the Olympic Games in Paris in 1924. Although the first race in 1925 went from Turna to Kosice, the traditional route has been from Kosice to Sena and back.

Eight Czechoslovakians ran the first Kosice in 1925 but were joined the next year by Hungarians, Germans and Austrians; in 1927 by Yugoslavians; in 1930 by Poles and Latvians; by Argentinians in 1933; by the Finns in 1934; Romanians in 1935; and by the French and the Swedes in 1937. By the time Buddy received his invitation in 1962, the Kosice Marathon was one of the most respected running events in Europe. Sergey Popov of the Soviet Union was the course record holder at 2:17:45, and Abebe Bikila at 2:20:12 was the defending champion.

Buddy did not change his training for Kosice, which would be held on October 7, 1962. The training remained a blend of hard interval work balanced by one long run per week.

· ·

Dear Fred,

I have just returned from Kosice. There is so much to tell I hardly know where to begin. The trip was the most fantastic experience I have had.

We flew from London to Prague and then took an all-night train to Kosice. I did not sleep a wink. When we arrived in Kosice, they presented us with flowers and a band played. Everywhere we went, people followed us asking for autographs and so forth. We were really given the "very important people" treatment. I did not notice much propaganda, although it was evident in some of the speeches. I was careful not to say anything which might be interpreted adversely in my conversations. I was told that I was the favorite (aside from the Czech, Dr. Kantorek, who won in 1958) with the people. I do not know if this was true, but I got off to a good start by kissing the pretty young girl who presented me with some flowers when we first arrived, much to the delight of the crowd.

One old Czech boy came up to me before the race and said quietly, "You know, the people will shout like crazy for Kantorek to win, but in their hearts, they want Edelen to win." I thought it was very nice of him to say this.

On race day, the weather was very, very windy (30-35 mph). The sun was on us all the way, and only the strong wind kept the sun from taking its toll. I ran steady (with the wind) all the way out to the halfway point in eighth position and moved to fifth at the start of the return journey.

They televised the entire race and blocked the route from traffic. As we ran along, thousands of people jammed the course and they had a band playing at various places as we passed by, including the turnaround.

I caught the leaders soon after the turning point. Paavo Pystenen of Finland led, but after 1 1/2 miles of the return I took the lead, tapping the Finn on the rear to let him know I realized he was doing the donkey work in pace setting, and that I was willing to have a go at the leading. The pace had slowed so I picked it up again when I led. After three miles or so of leading, I was tired a bit and looked behind to discover four runners behind me in single file to shelter themselves from the terrible wind.

I was a bit angry that no one else would share the work of leading. I almost stopped and, reluctantly, the Dane Thyge Torgerson took the lead. But the pace was dragging and I feared others would soon catch us and I'd be caught in a fast run from five miles out. I took the lead again and after a mile or two relaxed the pace to see if anyone else would lead. No one would. Finally, being really teed off, I took over and poured it on. I led all the way thereafter and in the last four miles dropped everyone but the Czech, Dr. Kantorek.

I almost dropped him a mile from the finish (had him by 30 yards) but then tired badly soon after. He came back at me. We entered the stadium, which was filled with 25,000 spectators, together. As we did, six men with trumpets began to play and two bands started up as well. It was very impressive!

Kantorek and I matched stride for stride around the track (650 meters). I felt sure I could outsprint him to the tape and was a bit too tired to make an all-out effort with 440 yards to go. Then, with 100 meters to go, he shot ahead like a bullet. Although I pulled him back the last 50 yards, he beat me home in 2:28:29.8 while I ran 2:28:31.4.

I was very happy to be second, but upset for allowing myself to be beaten. I could have tolerated a much faster pace throughout the race and was very disappointed because nobody wanted to come up and fight me for the lead. But that is the way of racing.

The wind and sun cost us a good five to seven minutes in the final time. Britain's great marathon runner, Peter Wilkinson, had an off day and finished seventh. The 1960 Olympic champion, Abebe Bikila, was not here although 12 to 15 countries were represented. Claus Moser of Germany was third as 78 finished.

I hadn't finished more than five minutes, and just had time to jog a lap with Kantorek, when they rushed both of us to a room,

weighed us to determine weight loss during the event and put us on
couches where they strapped cords to various parts of the body to
check pulse, blood pressure, etc. All this was carefully recorded. The
bloke who was doing these said to me: "Very, very good." I presume
he meant that I was fit. I lost 8.8 pounds during the race. I was 148 1/2
when I started and slightly less than 140 when I finished.

Incidentally, I did not drink any water during the race, but
sponged with water whenever possible. Consequently, unlike the
Poly and Welsh marathons, I did not have the slightest bit of stomach
trouble. In both of my other marathons, I had stomach trouble shortly
after drinking water. I feel you are correct about the necessity of
drinking water during the marathon, but it must be done in training so
as to become accustomed to it. Otherwise it may represent something
foreign to the system and act as stress instead of being beneficial.

After the race, we were taken to huge baths which were
heated to the same temperature as ordinary bath water. We swam in
there for a while and then swam for 15 minutes in another large pool
at a cooler temperature. Finally, two men massaged our legs (one on
each leg for some 20 minutes with soap). Surprisingly, I had far less
stiffness and soreness in my legs than I usually have following my
weekly 23-mile training run. It was amazing!

Following the post-race dinner, we went to a huge hall where
they had a variety show in our honor. They sang folk songs and did
Slavic dances. They had a large orchestra and dedicated songs to the
first three finishers. They announced they were going to sing "Swanee
River" for me. I then stood up and took a bow, which seemed the polite
thing to do to show my appreciation.

We took the train back to Prague and despite another sleepless
night I am pleased we took it. We almost flew from Kosice to Prague
but because of the fear of fog and the fear that we might miss
connections we took the train. After I got back to England, I opened
the paper to find that the flight we would have taken crashed and all
24 persons on board were killed. How is that for fate? It scares me to
think of it. Thank God for Czech trains.

I enjoyed myself to no end and, as I say, I am sure I made a

Gracious in defeat, with Kosice winner Dr. Pavel Kantorek.

good impression. I was interviewed for about 15 minutes for the television and radio after the race. They wanted me to tell a bit about how I started, where I went to school, how long I had run, etc. A few said to me that I was silly to lead practically the entire distance into the wind coming back. They said Kantorek ran fifth in the group of five that led on the return trip. "If you had done this you would have won." I guess a bloke just can't win.

I knew I was breaking the wind for the rest, but no one would lead at a decent pace and on a few occasions when I did not lead on the return trip we were almost jogging. It was true, however, that the strong wind cost me the race. I spent too much energy running into it. But despite this, I am told, I gained a lot of respect by taking the lead and speeding things up. I think maybe as far as the Czechs are concerned they like me more by just getting beaten than if I had won. I wouldn't have been nearly as popular had I won. I am now set for next year, and I hope the Japanese will invite me for their December marathon.

Buddy

CHAPTER TWELVE

*"Kantorek hung on
and we entered the stadium together."*

Until injury or indifference intervenes, good racing and good training spiral. Because a runner trains well, he races well. Because he races well, he trains well.

After Kosice, Buddy accepted an invitation to run the Asahi Marathon in Fukuoka, Japan, on December 2, 1962. In the interim he trained and raced in the spiral. One week after Kosice, Buddy took a 3.5-mile leg for his new club, Hadleigh, in the Hadleigh Road Relay. He broke Mel Batty's circuit record by running 15:54, a performance that stood as the best of the day, as Buddy wrote Fred, for about 30 seconds until Mel finished with a 15:34 for his team. Nevertheless, the run was satisfying, following as closely as it did the marathon in Czechoslovakia and the travel back to England. Buddy recovered rapidly from the run and was ready for more.

The next week he ran a five-mile road race at Romford in 22:52 and recorded that he "bashed it all out every step of the way." The run drew Fred's favorable response: "I like the idea of your running these unimportant races. Keeps you sharp and alert, serves as a fast, long, continuous workout. You don't need 5 x 2-mile workouts if you run these races." Buddy responded to Fred's approval with a four-mile relay leg in 18:52, the fastest clocking of the day. As often happened when Buddy trained hard and raced frequently, he noted that during this run he was tired but moved easily all the way. His mechanical efficiency, the ability to turn it over, was up.

As Fukuoka approached, the training and racing continued seamlessly:

Sunday, November 10: approximately 4.5-mile
cross-country race at Chigwell; first in 18:39.
"I really flew today.
I felt fabulous all the way. I ran hard but within
myself."

Monday: a.m. 21-22-mile run in 1 hr. and 56 minutes:
"I seemed to move easy all the way."
p.m. one-mile jog followed by 10 x 110 accelerating
sprints, with 30-to 50-yard jog after each;
one mile home.

Tuesday: 4.5 miles at race pace, home from school.
Light weights including dead lifts, curls, bench press,
hops with weights and semi-squats.

Wednesday: a.m. 4.5-mile run at quick pace
to school.
p.m. 4.5-mile run home moderately fast (5:30 pace),
followed by 3/4 mile to sea front and 30 x 440
at approximately 69-70 seconds each with
60-second jog after each: "I felt quite good tonight.
I was a bit tired on the early ones, but once I got
completely warmed up I felt very good. I have
steadily increased these reps. on the roads since
Kosice, and I have repeated the 30 x 440 now twice."

Thursday: a.m. 4.5-mile run "quite hard all
the way" against a cold wind.
Noon: one-mile warm-up followed by
30 x 110-yard accelerations, 110 jog between each
110 run and 3-min. jog between the sets of 15:
"I found it tough to go too fast on the first few as
the legs were a bit tired from the 440s last night.
However, the second set was very fast."
4 p.m. : after a half-mile warm-up,   15 x 110 very fast:
"every one was flat out." Then 4.5-mile run home,
 just "flowing along."

Friday: 4.5 mile very, very slowly to school:
"The only reason I ran today was the fact that I ran
home last night for my second session and so I had
my clothes at school. I found it much quicker to
 jog to school than wait for the bus. I felt not the
slightest bit tired today. With this jog I will definitely
not run tomorrow after travelling to Brussels. I have
virtually two full days now to rest. I think I'm headed
for quite a good race. I should run my best in International cross-country race. This race in Brussels,
I have heard, is the biggest of the Winter Internationals.
A good field is entered."

Saturday: rest.

Sunday: In Brussels, Belgium, for the Criterium
Des As (Race of the Aces).

"9.5 kilometers. Place: 4th. Comments: I was very pleased
at my performance today.   I ran very well, I thought, and more
important it was the easiest international cross-country race I have run.
I found the start too fast, but soon got up to the leading bunch
(Roelants, North, Bernard, Van Derwattyne and some Germans).

Roelants broke away about the halfway point and I tried to go after him with Gerry North, but found the pace too fast. We did four small laps and one big one. On the big one, with 1 1/2 miles to go, I managed to catch Bernard (France), who had gone ahead earlier. I passed him and caught Van Derwattyne. The last 880 I had a terrific battle with the latter. Roelants was first with North a second behind. Vandy was third and I was fourth by a second. Van and I came up to the last 440 side by side. I had managed to hang on despite his spurts. I surged ahead the last 220 with everything I had and got 10 yards clear, but he came back just as we entered the chute. I don't know how he caught me as I must have run my last 440 well under 60 seconds! I guess I should have gone with 3/4 mile to go."

With the race in Belgium behind him, Buddy took the last set of shots for travel in the Orient and anticipated Japan.

. .

In some marathons, notably Boston, where the terrain tempts a runner to recklessness with early downhill splits before introducing the hills between 16 and 20, the course is a compelling factor, an unregistered, unnumbered participant on race day. In Fukuoka, on the other hand, the course in 1962 was unobtrusive, flat and grey, out and back.

The Asahi Corporation organized the marathon in Fukuoka in 1947 as a means of encouraging post-war activity. Foreign runners were invited in 1954 and thereafter the race grew in stature. Before the line between amateur and professional was blurred to indistinction, and it took hard cash to persuade an amateur athlete to run an event, Fukuoka ruled because it was willing to pay a runner's way to and from the race and to treat him like royalty while he was there. An invitation to Fukuoka meant that a marathoner had arrived in the first rank.

The run started for years at the Heiwadai Stadium, skirted Hakata Bay on the way to Gannosu, turned there and returned home. Traditionally the 26 miles of running was watched and cheered by hundreds of thousands of spectators. The stadium was packed for the start and finish.

. . .

Dr. Pavel Kantorek ran Fukuoka four years in a row prior to 1961 and each time finished among the top four. Finally in 1961 he won. He was back to defend in 1962. At that, he was a long shot because the Japanese were ready. They looked expectantly to Takayuki Nakao. Nakao trained in New Zealand and while there won the Auckland Marathon in 2:18:52, ahead of two countrymen also entered in this race, Toru Terasawa (2:19:15) and Nobuyoshi Sadanaga (2:20:30).

Five other foreign runners joined Kantorek: Ivan Keats of New Zealand, Mamo Wolde of Ethiopia, Tenho Salakka of Finland, Choi Chung Kim of Korea and Buddy Edelen from the United States. Because of the Empire Games, no English runners were entered.

Buddy flew from London to Tokyo and on to Fukuoka on November 28. In the three days which remained before the race, he jogged and consciously ate enough to sustain him for the long run on Sunday, December 2, 1962.

. . . .

Fifty-four runners started from Heiwadai Stadium at noon. The temperature was a perfect 53 degrees F, with humidity in the low 80s giving way to rain as the bunched runners neared 10 kilometers. Ethiopian Mamo Wolde made the first move five kilometers later, darting away from a large lead pack. He took two runners with him, Toshimitsu Teshima and Asanari Sakai, but left even them at 19 kilometers. Wolde reached the turn with a 200-meter lead in 1:09:00. Sakai, Terasawa, Makoto Nakajima, Kazumi Watanabe, Kantorek, Kim, Salakka and Buddy followed. Wolde, however, was out too fast and the field knew it. Wolde came back and they accelerated toward him. By 24 kilometers the lead was down to 20 yards. Moments later it was gone: Nakao, Terasawa, Watanabe and then the deluge.

Keeping the pressure on Dr. Kantorek in Fukuoka.

With Wolde engulfed, Nakao carried a stronger rhythm, to which Terasawa and Watanabe responded. Buddy did not. He was already at the edge of his confidence and he dared not go faster. Watching the three Japanese move away, he could only hope that they would suffer greatly and return.

The three leaders passed 30 kilometers in 1:37:33. Buddy went through in 1:38:25. The marathon is a long way, it goes without saying, and Buddy knew he could still win. It was possible. But as the front runners worked together, joined in the later miles by Kenjii Kimihara in his first marathon, the prospect became remote. Even as he scanned the horizon for any hopeful sign, what Buddy heard behind him was the more pressing matter. The footsteps were no less disturbing for being familiar. It was Kantorek and in hindsight it should have been expected. They were so close in Kosice, why would today be any different? There was nothing to be done but stay with it, keep the pace steady and hard and trust that he could dislodge the Czech. Even at that, however, Buddy held something in reserve, just that one acceleration tucked away for later use. Buddy was educable.

Over the last eight miles the Japanese sorted themselves out, with Terasawa winning in 2:16:18.4 over his favored countryman Nakao, who ran 2:16:53. Kimihara finished third in 2:18:01.8 while Watanabe fell back through the field. Some 50 seconds back of Kimihara, Buddy approached the stadium with Kantorek still clinging to him. Buddy was tired but he was fully engaged, alert and ready. One thought—"not this time"—became controlling as Buddy entered the stadium. Buddy heard those words and he felt them. It was not right, not sporting, for one athlete to trail another so resolutely, to do so little of the work, and then to accept the reward of higher place. Buddy repeated his three words. It would not happen this time. Not this time! What 26 miles of steady running would not do, 385 yards of frantic, leg-worn sprinting would.

Inside the stadium, Kantorek moved but Buddy moved too, at once, and virtually simultaneously. Without the little jump he got at Kosice, Kantorek could not make it past. Buddy held fourth place from the doctor by two strides, 2:18:56.8 to 2:18:57.4. In two marathons the two men had run more than 50 miles together on two continents and cumulatively only tenths of seconds separated them. They were even now, one to one.

The first five finishers in 1962 broke the course record of 2:19:03 formerly held by New Zealand's Olympic bronze medalist Barry Magee. For Buddy, the result was a milestone. Nine years after Jim Peters first ran a marathon under 2:20, Buddy Edelen became the first American to do so.

· · · · ·

"Felt good to start. We broke up into two groups at about 10 km. I ran about 20th in the second group on the way out. Ran with Kantorek of Czech. I was concerned at about 12 miles that there were so many Japanese ahead, but at about 15 miles they started to come back. I had a rough patch from about 10-13 miles. My legs seemed to get a bit sore early in the race and the pace seemed a bit faster than I could manage.

"I hung on, however, and at about 15 miles I started to feel much better. I moved through the field and led a group of four. I began to run very strongly from 18 miles onwards into a head wind. Kantorek hung on me and we gradually moved up on the Japanese in front. I did not know how many were ahead. The last two miles I felt as though I was moving very fast. Kantorek hung on and we entered the stadium together. We strided around the track and I made a strong effort with 300 meters to go. He stayed with me until the last 100 meters when we both kicked for the tape. I pipped him."

CHAPTER THIRTEEN

"A day of rest might have been wise here."

As it happened it was neither disinclination nor injury that stopped Buddy's spiral. Returning home from Japan, he found 1962 giving way to the winter of 1963, full of snow, sleet and ice. The streets were treacherous and interfered not only with Buddy's long run but also with his extended interval work. Tracks, of course, were out of the question. As a result, Buddy concentrated on shorter, quicker runs and tried to get three sessions a day. He even moved some of the running indoors, using the school hallway for bursts of 30 seconds or so duration over and over and over. All he got out of that was sore calves.

Notwithstanding his trouble with the weather, Buddy raced well early in the year. At the Essex County cross-country championships on January 5, he waited with the other competitors while a tractor dragged the seven-mile course to make the deep snow runnable and then he took off, chased closely and finally overtaken by Alan Perkins on the first of four loops. After one, Perkins led him by four yards, which over the next three laps he attempted to lengthen with several bursts.

Four times Buddy dropped off the pace, stuck in the snow and apparently hopeless, but four times he got back up and closed. At the start of the last lap Perkins had only 15 yards to his credit and Buddy was hanging on, hoping for a bid in the last quarter. He moved there, in sight of the finish, but it took 400 yards of hard work before he edged ahead with 35 yards left. Unfortunately, as he did his foot slipped and Perkins on solid footing was in the chutes a stride ahead.

Buddy was exhausted by the run, too tired to care by the time it was lost. He took consolation only from the fact that he beat his friend Mel Batty, who came fourth.

· ·

The good run at Essex emptied Buddy's account. He overdrew it later in the winter, finishing well back at cross-country meets in France and Belgium before accepting what little respite this harsh winter had for him. On February 14, 1962, he flew to New York to compete in the New York Athletics Club indoor meet. The next day, running in the two mile, a distance now obviously too short for him, he chased Bruce Kidd of Canada through a 4:23 first mile before winding down to a finish back in the field, with a final time of 9:03. With that kind of time, it was college again! But he knew that his training had been haphazard coming into the event. In college 9:03 would have marked a peak; this year it marked a valley.

The night after the NYAC meet, Buddy was in Louisville, Kentucky, for the Mason-Dixon Indoor Games. Again over two miles he ran as fast as he could but not fast enough. On the oversized board track he finished second in 8:59, having run the first mile in 4:30.

The indoor meets out of the way, Buddy took the opportunity to visit Sioux Falls for two days, speaking on his last day to the local Chamber of Commerce, before travelling back to London via Minneapolis, Chicago and New York.

• • •

After running better than he expected on February 24 at a cross-country meet in Belgium, Buddy started the next day his big buildup for the spring. Although the cold winter persisted, the long run returned, the protracted intervals were revived and, to it all, Buddy added a sustained run on Wednesday evenings, usually 15 miles in approximately 1:20. Fred had advised for some time that the mark of the marathoner was two longer runs per week, and after 1962, it could no longer be denied that Buddy was a marathoner.

Although he continued to pay lip service to Fred's "gradual adaptation to stress" preaching, Buddy's mileage shot quickly up to 135 miles per week in March and held there. As the work continued, even Fred hardly knew what to think of it; how far could he let Buddy reach? One day he advised that volume was money in the bank and could not be avoided; the next he cautioned the need for two or three days' complete rest. As the spring continued, however, and the fast miles mounted, Fred grew more insistent that the risk of injury was now paramount. Especially as the AAA 10-mile championship approached on April 13, Fred urged Buddy to have "the courage to rest." Here was one contradiction Buddy never mastered, the need to rest to run. As a result, Buddy took his volume and little else to the defense of his AAA 10-mile championships.

Buddy had beaten Mel Batty narrowly the previous year but by now they were close friends. The two agreed to share the pace in the strong wind whipping across Hurlingham Park's cinder track. Mel led the first mile, too fast by any estimation, in 4:41.4, and Buddy took the field through two miles in 9:28.6. Mel was back for the third mile and Buddy the fourth. The three-mile split was 14:17 while four passed in 19:10. Five miles was 23:59.6. From there, Mel Batty took it on himself. Buddy could only watch as Mel moved away in the sixth, seventh, eighth and ninth miles. He finally pulled himself closer over the last four laps but it was too late. Mel won in 48:13.4 while Buddy in second place beat his time for the prior year by running 48:28.

Buddy in the failed defense of his AAA title, looking good
only on reflection.

Buddy with training mate, friend and rival, Mel Batty.

Mel's time was the third fastest ever run for the distance and might well have been a world record without the wind. Buddy's time was itself the seventh fastest ever run. Only Basil Heatley, Zatopek, Batty, Rhadi, Bikila, and Wolde had done better. As disappointing as this run was, it was gratifying to see an American represented in such company. And again the AAA brought new American records: seven, eight, nine, and ten miles as well as the 15 kilometer, the latter in 45:16.8.

The AAA having been run on a Saturday, nothing could keep Buddy from his Sunday long run. Joined by Mel, he ran 22 miles in 2:10. Throughout the period that followed, Fred's voice was in the wind: "No, No, No, I do not want to make you feel bad or hurt your feelings, but this (insert workout, from any number of days) is extremely poor judgement. This is the same problem we have fought about for years. The compulsion to run and restlessness come from mental inferiority complex. You were very unfair to Buddy Edelen."

With regard to the specific performance at the AAA Fred recognized that it was excellent running, but knew also that it was not what it could have been: "With the great volume you have taken the last six to eight weeks you are flirting with the brink of injury or breakdown. You would have run the 10 mile much faster with two full days rest, maybe more. Even though our objective is the Olympic Marathon title, Kosice, Athens, etc., there are times when you need complete rest." Reviewing the 22-mile run that Buddy ran the day after the AAA a powerless Fred just said: "Should have rested."

Finally on April 22, Buddy reported the inevitable. His knee hurt sharply during a long run of 21 miles. Fred tried one more time: "STRESS REACTION! Rest completely two to three days BEFORE it is too LATE! You are not too far gone yet but will be soon if you don't rest." Even at that, Buddy wouldn't stop running until he got in the Finchley Twenty, which he won easily on April 27 in 1:45:12. When the pain in the knee persisted after the race, Buddy finally stopped. He took three full days off.

Thereafter the knee hurt but not to the point of debilitation, and Buddy trained, more carefully now, for his next marathon.

CHAPTER FOURTEEN

*"Ran to a 5 km. schedule to break
the course record held by Bikila."*

To all appearances the Boston Marathon in 1963 had it all. It had Ethiopian teammates Mamo Wolde and Abebe Bikila pushing together through the Newton Hills; it had 1962 European champion Brian Kilby in hot pursuit and, finally, it had a sudden, cold wind from the east—into the face of the runners. The wind stopped the two Ethiopians, leaving the way clear for Aurele Vandendriessche of Belgium to move past Wolde at 21 miles and past a stiff-legged Bikila at Coolidge Corner to win in 2:18:58, a full 2 minutes, 11 seconds over local favorite and 1957 champion Johnny Kelley with Kilby third.

In fact, the Boston Marathon in 1963 was terribly flawed. With due regard to Johnny Kelley's excellent finish, the field lacked an American who believed and had proven that he belonged in this kind of company and who would go shoulder to shoulder over the breadth of the course and, win or not as the case may be, but would not be satisfied with pulling through the field late, as others folded in front of him.

Buddy Edelen was fit in the spring of 1963 and wanted to run the Boston Marathon. In correspondence with Jock Semple, he asked only what he required, air fare and expenses. Unfortunately Jock either spent what he had on Bikila, Wolde, Kilby and Vandendriessche or he had no money to begin with. In either event, he said no to Buddy and Buddy was nowhere near the Newton Hills when Bikila began to fade. He was home in Essex, preparing for the Marathon in Athens.

. .

Michel Breal of France suggested that the revived Olympics in 1896 include a run in memory of the Athenian soldier, remembered variously as Pheidippides or Philippides, who by some accounts ran from the Plain of Marathon to Athens to announce a victory over Persia in 490 B.C. Although the historical basis for the story is by no means certain, it had sufficient emotional content to warrant its inclusion in the program for Athens, the first host city. When a Greek, Spiridon Loues, won the event to the great exaltation of his otherwise empty-handed countrymen, the future of the Olympic marathon was fixed.

Imitative events appeared in France in July 1896, in Stamford, Connecticut, in September 1896, and in Boston in April 1897. From that base, the event, now standardized at 26 miles and 385 yards, has captured the imagination of runners and non-runners alike.

. . .

The International Classic Marathon from Marathon to Athens was run for the first time in 1955. Held biennially from 1955 to 1973 and thereafter annually, the race immediately attracted the best in the world. Even before Buddy stepped to the line on May 19, 1963, the winners included Veikko Karvonen in 1955, a year after his victory in Boston; Franjo Mihalic in 1958, the same year he too won Boston; and Eino Oksanen in 1959, who won the Boston Marathon not one but three times. Finally, in 1961 the classic distance over the classic course attracted the classic champion, Abebe Bikila. Bikila won in a course record 2:23:44.6, a record which Buddy coveted.

. . . .

"I think every marathoner should run the original course from Marathon to Athens. It's a tough one—by far the toughest marathon course I have run over. The locals claim you can cut five to seven minutes from your time due to the difficulty of the course but I don't know if this is true or not. The first six miles is reasonably flat but then it becomes hilly and you start to climb. The last six miles is all downhill but the race finishes in the stadium in Athens at an altitude higher than the start in Marathon.

"Before the race began, all the runners were given olive branches by the local priest and blessed. We then started, carrying the branches for some five kilometers to the tomb of Pheidippides, who first ran the course to bring tidings of the victory to the Athenians. As we approached the tomb, the many soldiers waiting presented arms to us and there was a big fanfare of trumpets. We then ran around the tomb, tossing our olive branches on it, and continued on our way.

"The weather for the run was pretty good. It was hot and sunny to start with but then clouded over after six miles. From about 12 miles it poured with rain for 15 minutes and I found it a bit miserable. My shoes were rather too large (to allow for feet expansion in the case of hot weather) and the rain got inside, causing me to develop blisters as my feet kept sliding inside the shoes. This did not last too long, however, as I gradually dried out again. The sun came out during the last eight miles, but it wasn't as hot as it had been during the first six.

"I had written out a schedule on the back of my hand and tried to run accordingly to break Abebe Bikila's course record of 2:23:44. I wanted to get ahead of the schedule for the first 15 miles and definitely for the first six. I knew if I could reach 30 kilometers on schedule I'd get the record.

"My plan worked perfectly. I led from about two miles on from John Stevens of Tanzania, who didn't fall back until six miles. Then I ran alone. I arrived at 30 km in 1:42, just as I wanted. I'm surprised my last 10 kilometers was not faster with the downhill finish

Alone in Athens, birthplace of the marathon.

Modest in victory.

but I did not kill myself. I slowed a little due to leg soreness from bashing the hills so hard earlier on in an effort to keep to the schedule.

"With maybe five kilometers to run, a young woman ran out to me on the road and handed me another olive branch. I had it with me the rest of the way and entered the stadium feeling very good indeed. I carried the olive branch over my head on the victory lap. My time was 2:23:06, breaking Bikila's record by 38 seconds.

"I was thrilled at winning this race. I had been laid low with the flu and in bed the week before and my confidence was a bit shaken. But apparently the flu did not hurt me and the enforced rest probably helped if anything."

CHAPTER FIFTEEN

*"On present form I feel
I will have a good run at the Poly."*

Athens had been the major event of the spring and it was won.
That being the case, Buddy approached the Polytechnic Marathon as
his next effort, but did so with lower expectations than usual. However
fast he might recover from Athens, one month between marathons was
pushing it. And one month is what he had.

Buddy did a little jogging one day after the Athens Marathon
and then rested three. On the fifth day, he jogged an easy five miles.
He thereafter resumed training as before.

. .

May 26: 22-23 miles in about 2:02. I was surprised
really this was so fast. It is the best time I have done
on the course; lst time (three weeks ago) I did 2:04.
I wore my Japanese "Tiger" shoes. I felt good running
in them; they are fantastically light and I have a
wonderful feeling of moving fast in them. My legs
were very sore from the pounding the last 10 miles.

WILT: Excellent. You need this WEEKLY.

May 27: 4.5 miles home from school at a fast pace.
My legs felt a bit sore from the long run and I did
not feel up to the fast sprints per schedule.

WILT: OK. This is using good judgement.

May 28: a.m. 4.5 miles to school fast.
p.m. 2-mile slow warm-up with a few fast strides
followed by 21 x 440 at 68 seconds each with 220
brisk jog for recovery. Mile taper. Ran these
with Mel Batty. I felt very good despite a nasty
wind. I could have done 25 OK but I was hurting
a bit on the last few to maintain 68s in the wind.
Am quite pleased with this session.

WILT: Just fine. Glad to see you back working hard.

May 29: a.m. 4.5 miles to school fast.
p.m. 15 miles in 1:19. I think this is one of the
fastest times I've done this run and especially
encouraging considering the wind. Legs felt
a bit sore from the pounding last four miles but
otherwise I seemed to move well.

WILT: This is terrific training.

May 30: a.m. 4.5 miles to school working at it but
slower than yesterday.
p.m. mile warm-up, then 7 x (stride 55 yards,
sprint 55, jog 110, sprint 110, jog 110, sprint 150,
jog 150, sprint 220 in 28-30, walk of two minutes).
Legs felt tired before this run. I think I attempted to

run all sprints too fast. I found the 220s were closer
to 30 than 28 seconds. I did not feel up to 10 sets;
my legs became too heavy. Still, it was a good
session. Finally, I did 4.5 miles home moderately fast.

WILT: Excellent. You do not need the 4.5 miles after
the sprints.

May 31: a.m. 4.5 miles to school moderately fast.
p.m. 25 x 440 (73-75) with 50-second jog; mile taper.
This was a better workout than it seems. I ran on the
King John School "roller coaster" and had a strong
wind against me on the uphill 220 part. These were
easily worth 71-72.

WILT: Remember, the big races (i.e. on the track) are
approaching and your volume must be CUT in favour of
QUALITY plus rest. But this workout is OK.

June 1: Mile warm-up to park; 3 x (10 x 110-120
very fast with 110 jog after each); three min. jog between
sets of 10; mile jog home. I found the sprint session
on May 30th left me a bit stiff and the 220s were not
quite fast enough. I did these in sets of 10 to do them
faster. Also, this is why I did not attempt more.
Went for a 15-minute swim in the sea following
the workout. I have been having trouble with blisters
lately and find the salt water does wonders for them.

WILT: Good judgement; I think the swim is just fine.

June 2: 10-11 miles steady on road. Decided against
the long run today. There was a terribly strong
wind blowing and I felt a bit tired. I could have done
the long one OK but I don't think I'd have gained

much from it. Instead I merely ran along as I felt.
Swam in sea after run.

WILT: Good judgement; the swim is fine.

June 3: Went for my usual 22-23 mile run;
about 2:03-04. The wind was terrible again. It was
with me going out but a standstill at times. Felt
good otherwise. Following the run, I went for a
15 minute swim. The salt water following
a hard session is wonderful for the muscles and blisters.

WILT: Good workout. You need this once each week.

June 4: 3.5 miles steady to track; 7 x (55 jog;
55 sprint; 110 jog; 110 sprint; 150 jog; 150 sprint;
220 jog; 220 sprint, two min. walk). Heart returned
all right after all seven sets but my legs were
shattered. I found 30s difficult. My legs became
very heavy after no. five on the 220s and even on the
110s on the seventh. This seems to be a damn tough workout for me. Perhaps it is not wise to do it the day
following a long run. Ran 3.5 miles home at quite a
good clip and felt better.

WILT: When you get adapted to this you should jog equal
distance after each sprint. Perhaps no sprinting after long run
is best. Can you arrange to rest after the long run?

June 5: 10.5-11 miles in 54-55 minutes. I was quite
surprised that this run was so fast. I felt good all the
way except the first mile. Decided against the 15
miler today in view of tired legs yesterday.

WILT: Just fine; good judgement.

June 6: a.m. six miles working hard at it all the way.
p.m. 2.5 mile warm-up with some fast strides;
4 x (440 fast, 440 jog, 440 fast, 330 jog, 440 fast,
220 jog, 440 fast, 110 jog, 440 fast, five minutes walk).
Averaged about 64.8 for the 20 x 440. Mile taper.
I was extremely pleased; some were in 63. Ran
these with Mel Batty, who did three sets with me.
I found the last set damn tough and especially the
last two 440s in each set. It is a tremendous
workout, however.

WILT: I think this is one of your best workouts ever!
Terrific! You are in great form!

June 7: Mile jog to track; 20 x 440 (70-71) with
45-second jog between each; 1/4 mile home. Felt
a bit tired from the speed session yesterday, and in
view of the warm weather, etc., decided on a quick
session of moderate 440s. Could have done 25 OK
but we have a meeting tomorrow.

WILT: Good.

June 8: Club meet at Harlow. Two mile warm-up;
 mile (2nd in 4:23); 30 minutes later the 880
(3rd in 2:07); 20 minutes later a 110-yard leg on
the 4 x 110 relay. I felt a bit tired today and the
weather and conditions were not conducive for fast
times. These runs took little out of me and provided
some fastish running for me.

WILT: Good effort.

June 9: 22-23 miles in approximately 2:01.

This is the fastest I've done this run. Ran with Mel Batty
who dropped back at 15 miles. I was more than
pleased with the time in view of the warm weather.
I had one rough spell at 15-17 miles when the sun
felt especially warm, but after that I caught a cooler
breeze from the sea and felt quite good. On present
form I feel I will have a good run in the Poly.
15-minute swim in the sea after the run. I am less
stiff after today's run than I have been in ages.

WILT: Great. You are in terrific shape.

June 10: 4.5 miles home from school working all
the way at it. 15-minute swim in the sea. The legs
were a bit tired—no more than usual, however,
following a long run. Felt much better following
the swim.

WILT: Excellent judgement.

June 11: a.m. 4.5 miles to school quite fast; felt good.
p.m. Two miles of slow jogging and 5 x 100 strides,
followed by 25 x 440 (67.4) with 220 jog in just
under 60 seconds; 880 taper. I am very pleased
with this session. I trained with Mel Batty and
felt quite good. We alternated the 440s and the
slowest was 68.0. The fastest was the first (66.7).
I could have ground out 30 but decided against it.
Covered about 17-18 miles today.

WILT: Good judgement in view of the forthcoming Poly
marathon. Otherwise, I would prefer the 4 x (5 x 440 at 63).

June 12: a.m. 4.5 miles to school quite fast
(bit tired in the legs).

p.m. 11 miles in approximately 55-56 minutes.
The legs were a bit tired from the fastish 440s
yesterday, but it was the sun and heat which made
the evening run hard. I could have waited until it
cooled off, but I wanted to run when it was warm
to get used to this heat. It appears it will be similar
in the Poly. 15-min. swim after run.

WILT: OK.

June 13: rest.

June 14: rest.

June 15, 1963: The 50th running of the
Polytechnic Harriers Marathon, Windsor to Chiswick.

CHAPTER SIXTEEN

"This is athletic immortality."
Fred Wilt

Although wind, temperature, altitude and surface, among other things, affect the relative worth of a run on the track, the course is level. For that reason if for no other, world records are recognized at standard distances on the track. Because the actual terrain varies in the marathon, however, traditionally no world records were recognized. Nonetheless, perhaps in recognition that the single variable of topography should not be sufficient to distinguish road from track, world "bests"were noted, as a means of charting rough progress in the event if for no other reason.

More recently, as road running boomed in popularity, the organizing bodies have struggled to bring some meaning to the times recorded in the various events. In the United States, for example, The Athletics Congress [TAC] passed new rules in late 1989 which eliminated from "record" consideration those courses which have a net decrease in elevation from start to finish exceeding one part per thousand (i.e. one meter per kilometer) and those races in which the start and finish are more than "30 percent of the race distance apart, as measured along the straight line between them," except "when it can be shown that the average component of the wind direction for the duration of the race did not to any extent whatsoever constitute a tailwind." When the 1989 rules were challenged--notably by support-ers of the Boston Marathon who resented the omission of perfor-mances on their course from "record" consideration--the Road Run-ning Technical Committee of TAC proposed refinements: a. the of-ficial performances listed by TAC will include both "record" and "best" times for each event; b. when a performance is listed only as a "best," the factors justifying that designation will be explained; and c. point-to-point courses which do not exceed the elevation drop limits will be eligible for "record" performances unless it can be shown that "substantial advantage was afforded the runner due to a significant tailwind on the course at the time of the race."

While such refinements are well-intentioned attempts to "level the playing field," so that performances can be realistically compared, they must surely fail. The courses in question are not level and never will be, no matter the rules and no matter the designations. Difficult courses and easy courses will fit coincidentally within the criteria established for "record" performances; and difficult courses will be dismissed from record consideration, as the Boston Marathon apparently is, even though any runner who has had the misfortune to pound down, and then up, and then down the hills in Boston will recognize that "net elevation drop" or not, that course can kill you. The only sound conclusion is that controversy will continue and it will remain difficult to know who holds the "record" for any road run, including the marathon. Ultimately, it may be necessary to recognize that arguing the relative merit of performances is part of the sport, and not unhelpful in maintaining interest.

Whatever the semantic difference between a world record and a world best, and whatever steps are taken to reconcile them, the modern marathon must begin with Jim Peters. When Peters found his stride in 1952, the fastest marathon ever run over the standard distance was that of Yun Bok Suh. Bok Suh was a shade over 5 feet tall and unknown before the Boston Marathon in 1947. In Boston, he gave Heartbreak Hill new meaning by encountering at that point a terrier run amok. The terrier knocked the tiny marathoner down. Picking himself up, Bok Suh gave such flight in his attempt to overtake the Finn Mikko Hietanen (and presumably to get away from the terrier) that he set a new record for the course, 2:25:39. It was the fastest time ever run for the marathon distance, eclipsing the 2:26:42 of his countryman Kee-Chung Sohn, who set his world best while contesting the Japanese National Marathon Championship in 1935 and, a year later, was required to compete for Japan at the 1936 Olympic Games in Berlin as Kitei Son.

Peters started his assault on the marathon world best at the Poly in 1952 by lopping five minutes off Bok Suh's time to finish in 2:20:42.2. Returning to the Poly in 1953, Peters ran 2:18:40.2. Six months later he answered the critics, who explained his fast times by pointing to the quick Poly course. He ran 2:18:34.8 in Turku, Finland. Finally Peters returned to the Poly in 1954, only two months before he collapsed in high heat while running the British Empire Games and retired from the sport, and knocked the record to 2:17:39.4. In four good runs, Peters had taken almost exactly eight minutes off the marathon world best.

Peters' last and best time endured until the 1958 European Championships. There the Soviet Union's Sergey Popov, a native of Irkutsk near Mongolia, disposed first of Alain Mimoun, an Algerian running for France and the reigning Olympic Marathon champion, and then of the record. Popov, at 5 feet 3 inches, ran 2:15:17.

Popov was the favorite for the Olympic Championship in Rome and he ran well there, going almost four minutes faster than the Olympic record. But he was fifth, as first the Africans swept away, the herald of a new age; and then Barry Magee, himself the representative of something new, the training method of Arthur Lydiard, which can be grossly summarized as long, steady running followed by prescribed periods of hill work and sharpening speed sessions.

In Rome, Bikila's winning time of 2:15:16.2 barely got inside Popov's best, but it remained the record for almost three years before Toru Terasawa of Japan ran a fraction faster in February 1963. Terasawa ran 2:15.15.8 in Beppu and it looked for a while that the marathon record had topped out. In the five years from Popov to Terasawa, including Bikila's stunning run in Rome, the marathon best had improved less than two seconds.

. .

After a lunch of cheese sandwich, ice cream and chocolate, Buddy had steak for dinner on Friday evening, June 14, 1963. He washed dinner down with three pints of stout and slept easily for 8 1/2 hours. Awake at 7:30, his pulse was 42 beats per minute. He had four soft-boiled eggs, four pieces of toast, a large cup of coffee with milk and finished the breakfast with two bars of chocolate.

His "fatigue index," designed to distinguish days on which he felt good, "one" on the chart, from days on which he felt bad, potentially "ten," was a two. He dressed casually for the marathon that afternoon, a white cotton T-shirt unlettered and many times worn, a pair of colored shorts, his light Tiger racing flats and a kerchief. He wore the kerchief as runners did on the continent, in four corners tied around the head like a bonnet. During the race, the kerchief was shade, rag and sponge in one.

Buddy had no particular plan for this marathon. He had trained well, and that gave reason for hope, even surprise. If it came, that would be good. But if it did not, it would be no worry. This race was extra, layered in on top of the Athens Marathon, which surely had been sufficient to hold his position among the best marathoners in the world and assure continued invitations.

Buddy went to Windsor Castle late on Saturday morning and picked up his number, 127. He pinned it in two places, left and right, on his shirt and joined the other 140 runners for the start on a day that was warm, at 73 degrees, sunny and still.

The field for the 50th running of the Polytechnic Marathon was unexceptional. The greatest threat appeared to come from Ron Hill, last year's winner, and from Alastair Wood, who had been fourth in the 1962 European Championship Marathon. No matter the nature of the entrants, the race lacked the preliminary excitement of last year's run because the Queen, to Buddy's disappointment, would not start the field. Instead, the starter would be Mr. Francis Neate, a representative of the company that sponsored the Polytechnic in 1963, Callard and Bowser.

At 1:30 p.m. the field moved away at Mr. Neate's direction. In recognition of the heat and the many miles ahead, the early pace was relaxed. Hill, comfortable in sunglasses and white cap, Wood, Juan Taylor, Roath, Shelley, Campbell and Collins joined Buddy through five miles in 26:15, a modest 5:15 pace. At his leisure, Hill occupied the time by telling stories about his child or some such thing as he ran. The others concentrated on the race, or tried affirmatively not to concentrate on Ron Hill's chatter, whichever method worked best to get the individual runner through the first few miles, so reminiscent of the early rounds of a prize fight.

By 10 miles, the pace was the slightest bit faster at 5:13 per mile, with a split of 52:20. At that, only four remained: Edelen, Hill, Wood and Taylor. As the four worked together and the field strung out behind them, the weather cooled slightly and a wind picked up, coming over the right shoulder of the runners. With each mile, the day became better for the running.

Buddy took water at every opportunity, because Fred had insisted, and waited for the right moment to move. He was more impatient than in the past because, as he realized with some amazement, he felt absolutely great! Following the natural rhythm of the marathon, the pace gradually increased between 10 and 14 miles. No runner among the four took credit for the push, but in all likelihood it was Buddy. Certainly by 14 he was in control, no longer able to deny a physical reality that increasingly said go. Wood fell back before 15 miles passed in 1:17:03.

Hill, Taylor and Edelen stayed together for another mile but by then they were not running together in any true sense. Buddy was pushing and the others were hanging on to him. At this point in the marathon, when a runner traditionally cautions himself that he has 10 to go, Buddy had the same thought with different emphasis: only 10 left! He moved from 5:13 to 5:04 pace through 16 miles and Juan Taylor flaked off.

Ron Hill remained, running lightly as always, a crowd pleaser with that smoothness. In six years he would twice run under 2:10 and take his place among the world's great marathoners. Today, however, as he threw off his cap and glasses he was unprepared for the leader's response. Buddy turned the pace up again, ever so slightly unless you're the one trying to follow it, to 5:03 and kept going.

Try as Ron might, Buddy Edelen moved farther and farther away from him. By 18 miles, Ron was alone and thinking of his own problems. Buddy was gone. Way out there on Ron Hill's horizon, Buddy continued to run swiftly, leaning back, holding his right arm at a skewed angle toward his body, pumping it erratically, and improbably covering distance. He was disrupted only when the lead vehicle took him 70 yards or so off the course. On another day that 70 extra yards would have been an irritant. On this day, it was insignificant. He forgot it as soon as it happened and was on his way toward Chiswick Stadium again. At 21 miles Buddy clocked 1:47:55 to Hill's 1:49:20. By 22 miles, the lead was a full two minutes and Buddy was still pulling. By then, he was toying with mathematics. He figured that if he was running 11 1/2 miles per hour, it would take Hill 12 miles per hour to catch him. He didn't think that would happen!

He was running so well that he knew he must be on to something and he was. Nearing the Stadium, he began to hear shouts from alongside the road: Go for the record, they shouted, each individually and then the next person down the line, a telegraph, all dots and dashes, of people with the same message. Go for the record.

Jim Peters' course record, Buddy thought, and he accelerated after it. Entering the stadium unruffled, he swung onto the track and ran the last lap near 70 seconds. Still feeling on top of his form, only a bit more fatigued in these last few miles, he savored the final homestretch, raising his arms high above his head in acknowledgement of the warm applause and the general enthusiasm the run had engendered. When he finished with a broad smile on his face, he continued straight into a combination cool down and victory lap.

Jim Peters was magic at the Poly and Buddy dearly wanted his record. As he warmed down, signing autographs along the way and posing for photographs, he waited anxiously for the time to be announced. When it was, he learned that he had Jim Peters' course record, all right. To his astonishment, he also had the fastest marathon ever run: 2:14:28. He had beaten Terasawa's record by 47.8 seconds. The marathon best which had inched forward less than two seconds in the prior five years had been well and truly smashed.

Ron Hill finished second to Buddy and ran 2:18:06, a time only Peters among Britons had beaten. Today, he could only wonder at the American and say: "I felt helpless as I watched Buddy go." Buddy's reaction to the time was about as clipped as his greeting to the Queen had been a year earlier, now six marathons ago: "Gee, that's great!"

More seriously, Buddy told the gathered sportswriters what his time really meant. "The days of the plodding marathon," he said, "are over. It takes speed work like the 110-yard sprints I practise and the hard training on the roads to give you both the pace and the stamina you need."

. . .

Poly Marathon . . . Place: 1st.

"Time: 2 hours 14 minutes 28 seconds. A new British all-comers, American, course and WORLD record!

"Happiest day of my life. I never dreamed I'd win or run so fast. I ran and felt good all the way. I moved with a tremendous mechanical efficiency. Ron Hill, who won last year, Juan Taylor and I ran together until about 15 miles when I just started pouring it on and left them. I felt rough the last few miles, but this was probably due to the fact that I have not covered a full 26 miles regularly in training. The race took little if anything out of me. I recovered immediately to jog around for a taper off. I simply cannot believe that I have broken the world record. Actually, we ran 70 yards farther than the exact marathon distance."

2:14:28

. . . .

No marathon world best would be complete without a measurement controversy. After Buddy's run, rumor had it that the course was, in fact, 103 yards short. For months, literally, organizers measured and re-measured before concluding that the route was 32 yards short, if at all. The confusion had come in reconstructing exactly where the race started. Once the tree in question, the one that marked the spot, had been correctly identified the rest was easy. The 32 yards was no problem, the press and everyone else concluded, because international athletics allowed one yard discrepancy for every 1,000 run.

Nevertheless Buddy continued to express surprise at the result. Interviewed for *Athletics Weekly,* he confessed that he "just didn't feel that (he) was capable of running 2:15. I mean 2:17, yes: 2:16:54 or something, possibly—but not 2:14:28, at least not yet. I could foresee it maybe in the next four or five years if I continue to improve, but when you get down below 2:20 you don't simply chop four minutes off your time in one race—at least you shouldn't do! This is why the time is such a shock to me." He added that he had noticed, "now that I've had six of them under my belt, that the worst part of the marathon, the last six miles, comes easier now. It's still tough, but whereas the last six miles used to be a matter of putting one foot in front of the other, now the fatigue and the pain is not quite so much. I feel as if I'm getting stronger and I can carry myself better and faster and smoother."

. . . . .

It would be easy to dismiss Buddy's 2:14 as serendipity. Just a good day, a gift from God that Buddy had the good sense to recognize and exploit. And that may in fact have been the case, given the dramatic improvement in his standard that the run represented. However, for these purposes, it makes better sense to look to Buddy's training and identify why he ran as he did.

In the first place, the harsh winter of 1963 forced Buddy to cut back, to take a rest he may have needed in order to incorporate the benefit of his past several years of virtually uninterrupted training. Suitably refreshed, Buddy could embark on his "big buildup," which packed prodigious speed and volume into a period of approximately 2 to 2 1/2 months. Third, just as Buddy may have seriously injured himself at the end of the buildup, he incurred a minor injury to his knee that required him to rest and thereafter to cut his mileage before Athens.

Athens itself will have contributed to the good run at the Poly. It confirmed his condition but did not take much out of him because by six miles in that race he was alone. As he often noted, he ran better when he was out front like he had been in Athens and he took less out of himself: "I have a greater mechanical efficiency—I seem to flow along— when I'm out alone. You can relax more, and that means you are conserving energy. When you're running with someone it's always difficult to know how much he has in reserve, how good he feels. But once you break ahead you know he's feeling pretty tough, or else he would come with you, generally speaking anyway."

Because he ran alone in Athens and won, which itself was a great boost, he recovered well. Five days after he ran it, five days of almost complete rest, he was back in training. He felt so good during the recovery that he considered a change of philosophy: "I used to think that you needed a minimum of six weeks to recover from a marathon and that three weeks was ridiculous because although physically you could be recovered, mentally you would not be prepared to put forth another supreme effort." Noting that he ran six marathons in the one year from June 1962 to June 1963, Buddy wondered whether his recovery wasn't assisted by the kind of training he did: "The way it's geared and the amount of mileage I do a week seems to indicate that I can bash out a marathon and recover in a matter of a few days."

It can be assumed that this view, whatever strength it may have had at the moment of expression, would be subject to modification in light of current opinion. Nevertheless the statement itself, made soon after the Poly, indicates that the recovery from Athens was,

After the finish of the world's fastest marathon,
Windsor Castle to Chiswick, 1963.

in fact, an easy one. In that event, the Athens Marathon, far from being a hindrance to success at the Poly, may well have been part of its make-up: a good hard run over the full distance followed by five days of complete rest before picking up the training again.

Additionally, the training itself between Athens and the Poly in 1963 shows the mix of speed and endurance work that Fred encouraged, long runs at race pace followed by sharp speed work.

Finally, and perhaps most important, Buddy ran well at the Poly because he was relaxed. He had already won his major event of the spring. He put this race on his schedule only because of its importance in the local running community, because of its grand tradition, because the course was near his flat and convenient, and, not incidentally, because he wanted to meet the Queen again, his only disappointment of the day. Whether he ran well was a matter of less concern than it had been in the past. This is part of the athlete's Catch-22 and this time it worked: Buddy created a scenario in which it would be unlikely that he would run well, the hard workouts on the Tuesday and Wednesday before the event being part of the scenario, and then he ran well. He must under that circumstance because he could not.

CHAPTER SEVENTEEN

"These bursts are dangerous, but much more
dangerous to others than to you."

Three days after the Poly Marathon, Buddy did his usual 4.5-mile run in the morning and later in the afternoon a hard interval session of fifteen quarters. By Sunday he was back to the long run, doing his 22-mile course in 1:59, the fastest he had ever done it. From that point, he trained steadily for his next goal race, the AAA six-mile championships to be held at the White City Stadium on July 12, 1963. The field for the six-mile run was stacked: Ron Hill, Basil Heatley, Jim Hogan, Mel Batty, Gerry North, Martin Hyman, Derek Ibbotson. Also entered was Brian Kilby, the newest marathon sensation for Britain, newer even than Buddy because Brian had responded to the Poly world best by running 2:14:43 in Wales.

The AAA six-mile was run on a rainy Friday evening. At the gun, Jim Hogan did the work. North, Hill, Heatley and Edelen bunched behind him while the rest of the field trailed in single file. Hogan maintained his rhythm with only minor variation, admitting only a lap's interference by Gerry North at four. When North slowed slightly Hogan went back to the front, a position he held until Ron Hill took over with six laps remaining. From that point, Hill surged once a lap in an attempt to shake Hogan. Failing that, he ran the penultimate lap hard and the final lap harder still, in 59.8, to lose Hogan and finish finally in 27:49.8, a mark which equalled the British Commonwealth, UK all-comers, UK national and championship records.

Meanwhile Buddy found Hill's pace too fast. He ran with Mel, with Basil Heatley and with Kilby for the first five miles in the second pack about 30 yards behind Hill and Hogan, and then tried to close up, leaving Heatley and Kilby but unable to make much headway with the two leaders. There was no drift in either of them. Over the last two laps, his effort spent, Buddy slowed. A third runner, Gomez, went by but no more, and Buddy finished in 28:00.8. Although fourth, his time was an American record by 21 seconds.

. .

Buddy had determined years ago that he could win a place on the United States team only by putting up some undeniable figures. He had done that now. Not even the AAU could ignore a 2:14 marathon and a 28 flat six mile. Buddy was added to the American team as a 10,000-meter runner for the upcoming dual meets with the Soviet Union and England, among other meetings. Unfortunately, just as Buddy got his opportunity he was in no shape to make the best of it. It was August of 1963 and he was midway between a full recovery from his two spring marathons and the fall marathon he had planned, Kosice. He was, in short, down.

And he stayed that way during the AAU tour. While English commentators felt strongly that he could run with the best the Soviet Union could offer, Bolotnikov being injured and unavailable, Buddy ran a disappointing race in Lenin Stadium. On a hot day, he felt awful, could not hold the pace and ended a non-scoring fourth and last behind both Russians and the other American. That really stung. After all the work he had put into building self-respect on the track and establishing his credentials, long distance, with the AAU, he had to run like that.

The rest of the tour was no better. Even against Great Britain in the White City, he ran badly, finishing in third behind Ron Hill and Basil Heatley. The tour mercifully ended after the run in London and

Buddy was able to turn his attention back to the marathon.

. . .

No good run over the marathon distance occurs by accident. By its nature it is the result of physical talent, mental toughness, appropriate training and proper attitude on the day of the race. Nonetheless, when a marathoner runs the fastest marathon of all time, the reaction is a mix of admiration and incredulity, with perhaps just a touch more incredulity than admiration. The incredulity focuses on the course, on the wind, on the coolness of the day, on anything that will cast doubt on the athlete's performance and provide a basis for discussion. Nothing about the fast run is beyond question.

The runner can respond to such talk in only one fashion. He or she must do it again. Only by repeating the effort will the happenstance and coincidence, the element of luck or chance, of wind and course, be removed. The second run legitimizes the first.

After a flight into Prague on October 11 and a sleepless, all-night train ride to Kosice, Buddy was ready to put the failed track tour behind him and end, once and for all, any doubt about his run at the Poly:

"I had trained for the Kosice race since August 7. I did not rest at all until two days before the race and trained twice a day all but three times, when I trained once a day. I had an indication that a good time was coming by the fact that I was recovering from day to day very well despite all the running and that I was clocking fast times over the shorter distances."

The field this year included Sergey Popov of the Soviet Union and it included a couple of Ethiopians, Biratu Wami and Demissie Wolde, who would be tough. Also, several top English runners made the trip, including Basil Heatley.

Buddy was comfortable in Kosice. He had built good will by his run the year before, the close finish with Kantorek, now missing by injury, and by his reaction to that close finish. He had been gracious and friendly throughout. This year he was the vocal favorite of the approximately 60,000 spectators who lined the course and of the additional 30,000 people favored with a seat in the stadium at the start and finish of this out-and-back event.

The race started at 1:00 p.m. on a warm, dry day, with winds at approximately 12 miles per hour, against the runners on the way out, theoretically with them on the way in. From the beginning the field moved without initiative over the cobblestones in the heart of the city. As many as 20 runners were still in the lead pack at 10 kilometers. Thereafter, as the field turned into open country, Heatley and the two Ethiopians moved to the front. They ran just fast enough to string out the pack until the 20-kilometer mark, when the Ethiopians applied the first significant pressure. From that point, the Kosice Marathon was a five-man race, with the Ethiopians running aggressively against Edelen and Popov, who struggled to stay in contention, and Heatley.

Buddy recalled the finish of the race in a letter to Fred, written

Bearing the sting of the Ethiopians' early running.

soon after the event. "On the return trip I ran with the Ethiopians, who kept putting in terrific bursts of about 150-400 meters in an effort to break away. I found each burst very tough but felt confident that they could not have prepared for this race much harder than I had. I therefore hung on each time. Finally, after about five of these bursts, one of them suddenly disappeared. I poured it on in an attempt to get away. I made about 25 yards but soon he came storming back up. He put in about five more bursts but after the fifth he made a motion with his hand, which seemed to indicate that he wished the pace to slow down. I interpreted this as a sign that he was tiring.

"By now I was quite tired myself but I decided to carry on with a burst of my own. I was soon free of the Ethiopians. Popov, of course, was well back by now. I felt good most of the way but found the last three or four miles tough. Last year as I approached the stadium, I thought I was getting away from Kantorek until I heard the crowd chanting his name, Kan-tor-ek! Kan-tor-ek! Kan-tor-ek! and I knew he was still there and that I was in trouble. This year they chanted my name and no other as I entered the stadium: Ee-da-len! Ee-da-len! Ee-da-len! It staggered me for a moment and then made me feel just great. I was all alone. No Kantorek this time. As I entered the stadium, I ran about a lap and a half with that chant, tired but satisfied and content. When I finished, a young woman threw a wreath of some sort over my neck and I carried it with me as I warmed down. It was huge but I managed it all right!

"The time was very pleasing: 2:15:09.6, which only I and Brian Kilby have beaten in the past. Actually, I would say that, taking everything into account, my time in Kosice was marginally superior to my Poly run. There was the travel, change of food, different country and the fact that it was an "out-and-back" course. The weather was also a bit warmer than during the Poly and we had quite a strong wind against us going out. Also, I personally found the cobblestones uncomfortable, although the asphalt surface on the rest of the course was good. The win and the time do a lot for my confidence. I feel now that I can run around 2:15 when really fit, and I think under ideal circumstances I should be able to break 2:14."

Buddy enters the stadium in Kosice with a record
that would endure until 1978.

. . . .

Buddy's time in the 1963 Kosice marathon broke Popov's course record, 2:17:45, by 2 1/2 minutes. The new record would last 16 years until 1978 when Chun Son Goe of Korea finally broke it by running 2:13:34.5. As for Popov in 1963, he eventually overtook the Ethiopians for second, running 2:17:45.2, while Chudomel of Czechoslovakia was third in 2:18:02. The ambitious Ethiopians finished 10th, Biratu Wami in 2:23:50, and 20th, Demissie Wolde in 2:28:39. Turning to old foe Basil Heatley of Britain, Buddy noted his place at fourth in 2:20:22.4 and said: "If Heatley put in some long runs and trained for the marathon seriously I'm sure he could get under 2:15." It was a prescient remark in view of what later happened in the Olympic Year 1964.

· · · · ·

"Buddy, were it not for the bursts the Ethiopians forced you to respond to, you might have broken 2:14! These bursts are dangerous, but much more dangerous to others than to you. Your training advantage is fast reps. of 110 and 220, with the occasional 440 reps. All of the top marathoners, such as Popov, are putting in as much total mileage as you.

"I think you have done a wonderful job here and have no complaint. Yet we must not be content or self-satisfied. We must ask ourselves where we could have improved. This does not mean you should have trained differently or raced differently. It merely means that we must think ahead and in advance of all others."

CHAPTER EIGHTEEN

"Ran with sweat shirts on to get used to the
warmer weather expected in Yonkers."

Thinking ahead, "in advance of all others," was Fred Wilt's hallmark. He might not always be right but he was thinking, and trying, keeping what worked, discarding what didn't and moving on to the next idea, loading one thought on top of another until he had what he needed.

When Fred met him, Buddy Edelen was a successful collegiate two miler. His success had come within the narrow confines of university competition, in the United States, over distances demonstrably too short for him. By 1963, Buddy Edelen had broken the American record at every distance on the track from six miles through the one-hour run; he was the only American to win a marathon outside the Western Hemisphere since Johnny Hayes' controversial victory in the 1908 Olympics, when Italy's Dorando Pietri wobbled across the line first but was disqualified for having received assistance; and he was the owner of the world best for the marathon, as well as the third best time ever run for the distance.

The progress had not come easy. It was in the first instance a matter of subjecting Buddy gradually to increased workloads and in the second of monitoring the workload to assure that it did not break Buddy down. In this second regard, Fred worried constantly about chronic fatigue and repeatedly asked Buddy to take complete days and sometimes complete weeks away from running, in an extreme version of "hard-easy" training. Fred also encouraged Buddy to monitor his pulse on a daily basis. The pulse indicated to coach and athlete whether the stress of the prior days was accumulating, such that the workload should be cut, or not, in which case additional work, in the absence of other factors, might be attempted. Fred also reviewed Buddy's diet and weight, which gave him an even more complete picture of the athlete's condition. Finally, from time to time, Fred recommended a blood work-up be done to further ensure that the body could accept the demands made on it.

To protect his athlete on race day, Fred advised Buddy to drink during his marathons, at a time when drinking liquid during a race was widely regarded as a sign of weakness and likely to result in stomach problems, the first of which objection Fred rejected out of hand and the second of which he eliminated by having Buddy drink on training runs so that he became accustomed to the experience.

Wilt was also open to unconventional ideas. Early in his relationship with Fred, for example, Buddy submitted to hypnosis in an attempt to help him run faster. The hypnotist planted the suggestion in Buddy that pain was a good thing, that when he felt it he should accelerate. It was a good idea but it was, over time, hard to tell whether it had any impact because Buddy appeared to act in that manner without regard to hypnosis. Buddy and Fred also experimented with "no breath" sprints, in which the athlete holds his breath during the course of a run. Theoretically a "no breath" sprint stimulates the build-up of lactic acid, such that running is uncomfortable, if not unbearable, and the athlete becomes hardened to the experience. This was another experiment that never caught on, but at one time Buddy could run 300 yards without taking a breath, a quirky accomplishment in its own right.

In all, the relationship between Fred and Buddy between 1959 and 1963 had been extraordinarily successful. As 1964 opened, however, the challenge for athlete and coach was even greater because 1964 was an Olympic year. And Buddy, as the fastest marathoner in the world, would bear increased scrutiny and therefore increased pressure. He had missed the team in 1960 at 10,000 meters, even though he was the American record holder in the event at the time, and he did not want that to happen again.

Buddy discussed the situation openly, as he decided how to prepare for the Trials marathon scheduled for May in Yonkers, New York:

"I may go back to the States in December to prepare for the Olympics. Being over here I might have a tendency to race more than I should, and I don't want to do what I did in 1960, running so much that when the Trials come along I'm just completely jaded.

"I was thinking of returning to Lafayette, where Fred lives, and doing my training there. I could get stuck into two or three months of solid training without the distraction of any racing. However, I will give this further thought; it's difficult for me to say at the moment. I didn't, of course, envision running 2:14. I'll probably sound Fred out a bit more before making a final decision. I know one thing—I don't want to race too much.

"Though I've got a world-best time it was made over a course which is extremely fast. I don't think you want to take too much stock of it. I wouldn't say that this time of 2:14:28, quite honestly, means that I'm that much more favorite to represent the United States at Tokyo than I was before the Poly. It probably scares hell out of my opponents but it doesn't increase my confidence.

"I know what it can take to spell the difference between a complete victory in the Olympic Trial race or complete disaster, and there is not all that much in it. It could be an injury three weeks before or it could be any number of things. When you have to come through on a given day or you don't go, the selectors don't care how many marathons you've won in different parts of the world.

"This is what I think is wrong with the selection system. Looking at my record so far, and if I continue to run as I have up till now, you would think that they would almost certainly pick me even if I did have an off day in the Trials. But they won't do that. People come up to me and say you're a certainty for a medal in Tokyo. I'm not even thinking of a medal in Tokyo. I'm thinking of making the United States Olympic team."

From this statement, made in the fall of 1963, it is evident that Buddy is following a traditional course: he demeans his own accomplishments as a way of lowering expectations and of keeping himself from overconfidence; at the same time, he suggests that his accomplishments are good enough that no trial should be necessary, such is his superiority to the other candidates for the team position; he swears off racing; and, finally, he vows to train with this one goal, selection, in mind without looking forward to the Olympic Games themselves.

. .

The first and probably the easiest decision Buddy made was to stay in England where he had a job that permitted time to train and travel; where he had good friends, notable among them the Ballards, who were members of the Hadleigh Olympiads and who often opened their home to him; and where he had a routine. Against all this, the benefit of any other venue, even in Indiana with Fred, was speculative. The Olympic year was no time for speculation.

Because he was staying in England, where opportunity would call at every weekend, it was particularly important that Buddy control his impulse to race. In light of this, the schedule after Kosice through early February 1964 calls to mind a binge drinker who knows that he must stop soon. Buddy ran 17 races in that period, including major and minor cross-country meets in England, minor road relays for his club, international cross-country meets in Belgium, France and Morocco, and a track meet in Morocco.

Of the 17, none carried the emotional burden of the Criterium Des As on November 24, 1963, in Brussels, Belgium. Days earlier Lee Oswald had killed John Kennedy in Dallas. When Buddy heard the news, his instinct was to withdraw. His second thought was to represent his country in Europe the best way he knew how—by running hard. He finished second in the race after a sleepless night.

. . .

The races in late 1963 through February 15, 1964, could be justified. Unless an athlete repetitively responds to pressure in secondary events he or she will not know what to do with it on the day that counts. By February 18, however, even Buddy recognized that he should concentrate his energy on the trial marathon, as he had promised he would. He started on that day two months of training in which he ran twice each and every day and moved the mileage, which roughly followed the previous pattern, over 135 miles per week. None of it was jogging.

On those rare occasions that Buddy was tempted to sneak in what looked like garbage miles, a seven-mile run at moderate pace, for example—Fred was there: "Buddy, you probably have some good reason for this particular workout. (But) it is not much like your usual training and it is not nearly enough in terms of either volume or intensity." As always, Fred's advice was to work or to rest, but not to put in a mile just to see it there on your diary at the end of the day. If Buddy could manage only a seven-mile run at moderate pace, Fred would prefer he rest.

Training in cool, wet England, what Buddy feared most was that the marathon trial would be run in high temperatures. He hated the heat and had suffered in it, most recently in Moscow. In December 1963, Buddy wrote a public letter to *Track and Field News,* expressing the "hope that the Olympic Committee would try and arrange the trial at a time when the weather roughly corresponds to what the U.S. marathoners will encounter in Tokyo. Likewise, I think the course (terrain) for the trial should be the same as the Tokyo course, e.g., it would be ridiculous to hold the trial in 85 degree temperature over a very hilly course if, in the Olympics, the temperature will be 60 degrees and the course dead flat." The magazine editors warned Buddy

The solitary long run on Sunday morning.

in response to his letter that the request was "too much to ask."

Ridiculous, Buddy had said, and ridiculous it would be, but that would not change the day or the result. Somebody would make the Olympic team in Yonkers in May, however hot it might be. With that knowledge Buddy and Fred planned for the heat even as they dreaded it. Buddy began training in three and four sweat shirts. Buddy gained advantage not only from the acclimatization but also from the extra resistance, i.e., the extra weight the sweat shirts provided.

As an added precaution, Buddy also began lengthening his long run. He started on February 23 with a Sunday run of 17-18 miles but soon went to the customary 22-23 mile run. Finally, after a few light days in mid-April, Buddy increased the run up to and then beyond the marathon distance. A selected eight-day period shows the nature of the pre-Yonkers work:

Sunday: May 23: Sunday long run of 28 miles in 2:39.

Monday: rest.

Tuesday: a.m. 4.5-mile run to school "working quite hard all the way."
p.m. 2.5-mile run to the track; a few fast 110 strides; 20 x 440 in 69-70, with 220-jog interval; 3.5-mile run home.

Wednesday: a.m. 4.5-mile run "working it all the way."
p.m. 15-mile run in 1:18.

Thursday: a.m. 4.5-mile run "steady to fast" against the wind.
p.m. mile jog; 25 x 220 fast with 220-jog recovery; 4.5-mile run home.

Friday: a.m. 4.5-mile run to school "steady, but
working it hard."
p.m. 10.5-11 mile run in about 58 minutes.

Saturday: a.m. 2.5-mile warm-up; 5 x 100-yard sprints;
10 x 700 yards in about 1:55 each with 350 slow jog
recovery after each. Mile taper.
p.m. 2.5-mile warm-up; 15 x 110-150 strides
on grass; 1.5 miles home as taper.

Sunday: 28-mile run in 2:36: "I lost a lot of weight
today due to the fact that I wore four sweat shirts and the
sun was out all the way."

Buddy trained in this manner until he left England on May 21,
1964, for New York and the most important race of his life.

. . . .

Buddy could thank the people of Sioux Falls, South Dakota,
and his own good sense in maintaining contact with them, for the fact
that he could even afford the trip to New York. On a teacher's salary
of $150 a month, he would have been hard pressed to pay the air fare
himself, and in 1964 the AAU did not help out. So it was up to Buddy's
friends to come through and they did, for which he was grateful.

The pressure on Buddy was tremendous as he headed "home"
to try out for the Olympic team. In England, all his friends and all the
experts, whose opinions he valued and whose respect he wanted very
much to keep, considered him a lock for a spot on the United States
Olympic team. If he failed now, would he ever be comfortable in
England again? On the other hand, even knowledgeable people in the
United States wondered about his credentials. When he left the
United States in 1960, he was a good runner but nothing great. And
the two times since then they had seen or had opportunity to hear first

hand of his running, he had shown little. During two indoor meets in 1963 he ran only as well as he had in college. And later in 1963, he had failed miserably on the European tour.

How would he be received now, he wondered. How would his accomplishments be judged?

CHAPTER NINETEEN

"In a group of four or so for the first 10 miles."

Buddy Edelen was a myth. Reports of his running came in from London, from the North of England, from Athens, from behind the Iron Curtain in Czechoslovakia and from Japan, but no one believed what they read, not even the men who wrote for a living. No American could run a marathon as fast as the reports said Buddy Edelen had.

Still, it was intriguing to think that it might be so. After all, no less a figure than Vandendriessche after beating the great Bikila in the 1963 Boston Marathon said that Buddy was the man he feared in Tokyo! It made no sense. It made even less sense when the Belgian said that with a favoring western wind Edelen could run Boston in under two hours.

What to make of it! He certainly looked a runner however. You had to give him that. At 5 feet 10 and trained down to a gaunt 138 pounds, geez there was nothing but sinew. But could he run in the heat? We would see; yes, we would see about that.

. .

In fact, this race in Yonkers, the doubters and instant marathon experts aside, was Buddy's race to lose. He was not myth and these runners had no right to stay with him. It seemed a harsh attitude and he was not proud that he felt it. But that was at the bottom of things. He had worked too hard, had sacrificed too much, for these runners to consider taking what belonged to him.

Nonetheless, he was worried. He had seen it coming and had trained for it. Four sweat shirts on a beautiful day in England had seemed paranoid. Now it looked like good planning. Still he had not believed it would be this bad. The forecast was temperatures in the 90s on race day and the start was at noon. At noon on hot roads, out and back along the river, with more than an occasional hill, people could die. That did not seem an exaggeration and sensible people, people who ran and who understood, urged AAU officials to change the starting time. But the officials refused.

With that, all of the runners would do the same thing. They would put the best light on it and try to forget, each of them, the memories they had of high heat. Buddy himself would forget the day he was roofing houses in the summer heat of South Dakota and ended up in the hospital for heat stroke and he would forget the woeful, disgracing run in Moscow. He would accept the heat, keep his head down, take water, concentrate on his strength and he would win. He had to win. His friends in Sioux Falls had paid his way and he could not, absolutely would not, disappoint them.

He was helped in his resolve by one comfort. Fred Wilt was in New York for the race. Buddy would do the running but Fred would be on the course to give what assistance and encouragement he could.

. . .

One hundred sixty-three men entered the Yonkers Marathon in 1964. It was three races in one actually. It was the annual Yonkers event and awarded the Metropolitan AAU championship; it was this year the National AAU Championship; most importantly it was an Olympic qualifier. One man, the winner, would be chosen for the United States Olympic team. The other two American representatives in the marathon would be chosen later in the summer at a race in Culver City, California.

The field of 163 included many with no pretense to victory and nothing Olympian in their considerations. Others did nurse such hopes. First of course was Johnny Kelley, the winner of this race for each of the last eight years, an Olympian in 1956 and 1960, a man described by the press as a cagey 33-year-old schoolteacher from Groton, Connecticut. Norm Higgins, Mike Igloi's athlete and reputed to be the best marathoner on the West Coast, was also in the field. Higgins could win if Buddy ran carelessly. And then came the Marine Alex Breckinridge; Gordon McKenzie, second in the Pan-Am Marathon in 1963; Hal Higdon from the University of Chicago Track Club; and the perennial Ted Corbitt, himself an Olympian.

The marathon course started at the War Memorial Stadium, traced one lap around the oval and then swung out onto Yonkers Avenue, down Walnut Street before turning north on Saw Mill River Road, on which most of the running would be done. Roughly, the course was out and back on Saw Mill River Road, hugging the Hudson River all the way: Yonkers, Hastings, Ardsley, Greenburgh, Eimsford, Mount Pleasant with a return. The course was supposed to be somewhat less hilly than previous editions but it still looked tough to someone running on it.

. . . .

At noon on May 24, 1964, in Yonkers, New York, the humidity was high and the temperature was 91 degrees. The surface temperature was 140 degrees. At the gun, 128 men from the entry of 163 set off.

The course was clear of automobiles in Yonkers. Thereafter the runners were on their own, dodging traffic coming from both directions. Few spectators lined the course.

. . . . .

Train the mind; the body will follow. Buddy had trained his mind; he was ready to drive. As he stepped to the starting line he gave one final remorseful glance to the clear sky. Then he let go. His mind slipped easily into a forced patter, the mind control that pumped positive thoughts to his body, obscured his fear, kept things moving and avoided panic:

"I have to admit it. No sense denying the reality. It is hot out here, hotter than I thought it would be. It's OK though. I love the heat. It's natural, and harder on them than on me. I like it; I'm part of it; very late in the game I can be part of it, indistinguishable from the heat, part of the glare. It doesn't matter to me. I hope the wind blows too; a sirocco, a regular heat storm. When it blows I'll be with it. Just stay relaxed. Very relaxed. Make your concession. Bend with it, stay with it. Be one with it; hold it where you are.

"Here we go now. Very relaxed. Let them fight the heat and the wind. You relax. Relax. Relax. Keep it steady. Blend in. Nice and smooth. This isn't your job; stay off the pace. Let the others do this now; you take care of yourself. That's the one good thing about a marathon. You don't have to break for the pole. I've seen some messes on the first turn. But this isn't it. No hurry now, not in this heat. Can you imagine starting at noon in this weather? Forget it. Just move along with this bunch.

"I know Kelley and Hal, here's Hal; he can't run with me. I don't think so anyway but he did run well at Boston. Breckinridge and Higgins up front. I've been gone a while ... don't know the others. Goodness but this is slow. Why doesn't someone pick up the damn pace? Can I run at this pace? Just awhile. Wait. There will come a time to run fast. But not now. Not yet. Just stay in here for a moment or two and let things shake out .

"There's Fred with the water. Take it. Take it early. This is the day to take all you can get.

"Buschman, Kelley, Allen, Higgins and Higdon. Names

through a split. Checking the runners through. This means nothing. It's too early. Some of these guys will be gone in a minute. They'll do it themselves. The rest are mine. I'll do what has to be done. For now, rest here. And stay very relaxed. But really this is too slow and I won't want to wait too much longer. I have no patience for this. I run harder on the way to school. Can't manage this much past 10.

"Here . . . here . . . 10 in Jesus Christ— 10— 55 minutes. I'll grant you it's hot but that is a ridiculous split. Ten in 55. Time to move. I'm not staying here any longer. Not at this pace. I know what's up. You lot think I have no speed, that you can hang with me for 26 miles and then outkick me for my spot on the team. Well, OK, that's fine, fair enough. Let's see how you like a 16-mile sprint. Move now. Not hard. Not yet. Just steady but faster than they can run. You move through now but don't press. Not quite yet. Just steady, steady, steady, steady, keep your jaw line loose; neck loose, eyes open and relaxed. Don't look to the horizon; it recedes, fades if you do. Just press ever so lightly but make it count. They can't do this. You can. You can. Nice and easy but make it count. Can you relax and run hard? Can you make it happen? Yes. You can. You're OK. This is fine, nice and easy. This is good. Steady running that's what we need. A tempo run. Nice in here but I want these guys to hurt. I dare them. This should be easy for you but they can't do this. Forget them. Concentrate on what you're doing. Keep moving now. Can you hear what's happening back there? I don't hear it. Are they coming? No, I don't think so. Not now. They don't want this. It's too far from home and this is just a step too fast.

"One step too fast every quarter mile or so and that'll do it. That's what this is all about. A step here and there over a long distance is a great gap. It separates people. A step. Here and there just a step faster. Really, one beat of the heart quicker than they can manage. Just one step, one beat, repeat it quickly, quickly, quickly but relaxed. They can't quite do this. One step. One step. One step faster every quarter mile or so and it can happen. You're a long way from home but you can do this. Just that one step, that one beat quicker. But it makes all the difference. It's Fred. All that damn speed work, I wondered sometimes; those 150s; the roller coaster; the pickups; the speed that these guys didn't or couldn't or didn't know to do. It gives you that one step, faster, over time. I don't hear a thing back there. I think they're gone. One step repeated; just one step over time in a cadence they can't quite match.

"I think you're alone. It's early and that's a little scary but I think you're alone. Alone. All alone and you do what you can. It's a hot day but it can work. Just keep going.

"You're away. You're definitely away. It's just you now. It was easy. Two miles of pressure after 10 and you're away. I make it a hundred yards or so. That'll do for now. They were afraid of you. Or was it the heat? They may have been afraid of the heat. I think you're OK but they may be right. They may be right unless you do this now. Run, press, lift, stay light but it is hot. It's OK and you've made a break here so don't let down but give a thought, just a thought now and again, to Dorando and then to Jim. Big Jim Peters in Vancouver in 1954. He could really roll but he damn near died that day. How hot could it have been in Vancouver? Vancouver for Christ's sake. OK, it could have been hot. He did look awful so it must have been hot. But not this hot. He couldn't have run in this heat. Not like you can. Nice. Very easy.

"It's good this heat. I think it actually makes the run easier, not because it's fun . . . it's not that . . . no, it's quite hot, I know that . . . but it scared 'em away and left it to you. And you can do this, training in four sweat shirts and the like. Oh for goodness sakes, keep your eyes open. It's one thing to squint the sting out of your eyes, but concentrate. I can't believe you. You almost fell off the road that time. Does this road have a camber? Here's the turn and you can see it now all the way back in.

"You're alone. But remember. This is one off. You can't finish second today. Second is last. Second doesn't get you to Tokyo. Second gets you to Culver City and you don't have the money to get to Culver City. Win today. You will; just keep moving. Look sharp. Ships in the night. They have nothing to do with you. Look good. Some of these people are in bad shape. Higgins looks OK though so stay on top of things. Put some of these miles behind you.

"You're getting tired. I hadn't realized it but you're getting tired. Get to 20. Twenty is the key. Get there. It's a long way from home maybe 18 and you're getting tired. At least try to run a straight line; level out; don't wobble; keep it even; keep it steady; move straight. Stay relaxed. You can do this but if you don't stay on top of things you won't do it. You'll lose it.

"On a day like this you have to stay on top of things. You can literally fall off the road. So keep moving. Moving. Moving. Nice and easy. And relaxed. How many times must I tell you. You're OK. Just easy here but concentrate.

"I could use a squeeze of water on the neck; a sponge get one at 20.

"Can you run hard from here? Yes, I think you could—but why do it? Just stay even. Take a little peek, see who's there. I'll bet no one is. They'd have to be pretty stupid to follow this rhythm. Only you can do this. In this heat. They couldn't or if they could they wouldn't dare. This is your race. My race. Our race. I'm getting a little silly in here. OK, here it is, not yet, not yet, not yet; all right, there we are. No one in sight.

"That was worth it. I feel better now. Just keep moving. You're alone in the heat. You know how this works. You get real tired but you keep moving and you win. You give the impression, if you can, of complete ease. Make it good. Make it easy. Just look down and keep moving relaxed, relaxed, steady, easy, put the miles, actually put the steps and half steps, behind you. This looks easier than it is. People expect this much, so much. All the training in the world doesn't change things. When it comes to this, it's all the same, it's hard. Ah, I can use that, a little patch of shade, get over there and use it. I'm not sure I can tell the difference but it looks cooler. It looks cooler. How many times can I say that to myself? It hardly matters. I'm moving and I'm alone and I'm staying relaxed.

"You know, this is done. From now on this is the way it goes. When I die, I suppose I will and if I don't keep my head down it'll happen today, they'll write it up: Leonard (Buddy) Edelen, 71,— no, that's too young. It seems old now but at 71 you won't be ready to give

it up. That's too young by far. You may even be running when you're
71. Give me a break. This is it—never mind 71. How about this? Like
this, this is it, keep moving— now you're getting a little delirious; who
can tell the difference? Christ its hot!

"And I'm not kidding; it's getting hotter. Stay relaxed.
Where were we . . .oh now yes: Leonard (Buddy) Edelen died quietly
(how quietly; what do you expect, to die noisily or with a great ruckus.
Man, this is getting to you)— Get back to it. What were you thinking?
Oh yea, this is yours. And this is the way it will be: Leonard (Buddy)—
I think they'll add the nickname, how could they not— Edelen died
today at his home in Rockhurst, New York— you've never even been
to Rockhurst, it has a nice ring to it though; I wonder if there is such
a town; I hope it's not near here; it's too hot around here— oh keep
moving and stay steady, no one's near but it is hot and you're a little
wobbly. I didn't mean it. Go on with what you were saying but keep
moving . . .died at his home in Rockhurst, New York, at the age
of 122 (yea that's more like it; you'll certainly be ready to go by
then; hell, you're ready to go now; what a day!). Mr. Edelen in
1963 held the world's best in the marathon at 2:14:28. Imagine how
fast they'll be running by then . . .but not on a day like this. This is
tough. A member of the 1964 Olympic team. Yea, that's the obituary.
After today.

"Twenty. Finally. I would have thought sooner but there it
is. 1:48. OK. That means nothing. Six to go.

"It puts a nice gloss on things. They can't take it away from
you. Making the Olympic team. There's Fred— get some water. A
sponge. Soak the kerchief. Hit the neck with it.

"Twenty-one bloody miles and I'm falling off the streets.
Wilt did this. I love him like a father but he did this and there he is.
How much farther!? How much farther?!

"I'm losing it a bit. That was unnecessary. It made Fred un-
easy and it wasted energy. You just have one job to do. You're a good
runner, well trained and moving well. You're way out front and you're
tough as nails. Hold this thing together. And try to do it with some
class. Look good. Look good. Stay steady. Make them understand,

130

make them know just how tough a bird you are. Indeed, I can actually hear each footstep. That's ridiculous. Each step. A nice quick movement. Actually not—but good enough. Keep your head down and keep going.

"This one hill. Do you have the courage to run this hill? To run it hard and steady. To render it mute. To smooth it out. Cruise it. Nice and easy. Relaxed. Relaxed. Why did they put a hill here anyway? Wouldn't even notice it in the car. I'll bet the hill was here already. That's a fact; it was here before they mapped the course. That explains it! Actually I don't want to complain but this is one hilly bastard. I'm doing the best I can. But these bloody hills. Not like back home.

"Kelley is gone. Higgins, Higdon, McKenzie, who were those other guys. That makes a nice little poem:

> Kelley, Higgins
>
> Higdon and McKenzie

"That's not a poem; it sounded good at first; like the start of a poem. But it ended up a law firm.

"Concentrate! You're alone but you're not finished. You're alone because you earned it. You can do this and they can't. You are one tough bastard. Say that over again and say it slow. Say it one word at a time. You, are, one, tough, bastard. I love these moments of congratulation. You are a stupid sod. Just keep running and save the back patting for later.

"A little more than two miles more of this. Then it's mine. Try not to close your eyes like that. Every time you do you almost fall off the damn road. That would look great . . . and it would change the obituary. Buddy Edelen, who fell in a ditch trying to make the Olympic team - what a jerk. This is what happened to Jimbo in '54. One moment you're there; the next you're gone. I've been drinking though. At least I've got that much. I can make it from here. I'm dead beat but as long as I keep thinking straight and concentrate. That's what it comes down to . . . with this long haul . . . all alone out here over these roads, no company, but really who wants it . . . it's concentration Keeping it steady, keeping it smooth; nothing wasted. Working the hills, maintaining your cadence; avoiding the bumps that cramp you; taking water where you can; the sponge on the back of the neck. The little things. They make it work.

"When I crest I'll see the finish line. Nope. Not there but soon. Very soon now. This is done. Don't know what the time is. Good but not sensational. Who gives a damn? Not me. Not this time. I've earned this. What a damn day! Too hot too windy too long too lonely! Yea, like you'd rather have company? No, this is your day. You should be alone. Finish alone. All alone. The toughest, maybe the dumbest, no the toughest, marathoner out here. And all alone, all alone. Me and Fred. Really, he's been most helpful, I must say. How much farther? He should hear that. How much farther!! Why do I keep yelling? It makes things such a panic.

"There it is then. There it is! OK, now it's done stay steady easy and so you are. I want your stride to even out. I want it to look like it did when you started. This is great. Just like that. Flatten this thing out and make it work. You did it. You did it! I can't believe you did it. But you did and here it is. You earned it too, what a day. Damned hot and only you. Nice and relaxed. Not too much now. I think Jim was on the track and you're that close now and he lost it. What a mess that was. So steady. Steady now. But no, you've got this now.

"You can do this. Just concentrate on what you're doing. No Dorando today. No Jim Peters. Just one relaxed, businesslike, yes that's a good way to state it, a nice, businesslike run for a nice fellow like you. What a guy!

"That's it then. Christ, it's done! They'll never, never take that away from you. Tokyo! Tokyo! Tokyo! And you earned it. What a day. I wish I hadn't taken that little bound at the end. A little more casual next time. Tokyo. Next time it's Tokyo!"

·   ·   ·   ·   ·   ·

Buddy Edelen won the trial race in Yonkers in 2:24:25.6. His closest pursuer was a man named Adolph Gruber, an Austrian who expected to run in the Olympic Marathon for his native country. Mr. Gruber finished almost 3 1/2 miles behind Buddy on this hot day,

Buddy Edelen wins the 1964 Olympic Trials Marathon in scorching heat.

recording a finishing time of 2:44:11. Johnny Kelley fought Gruber to the end but finished in third at 2:44:46.4. Norm Higgins, Buddy's closest competition at 15 when he trailed by only 100 yards, trailed subsequently at 20 miles by four minutes. Then he blacked out and ran into the side of a building.

Of the 128 men who started the marathon at noon from the old stadium, only 37 finished within the four-hour limit established by race officials.

To his friends, the Ballards, waiting back in England, Buddy sent a telegram: "Tokyo bound. Won by 20 minutes. Temperature 95 Fahrenheit-thirsty as H." He signed the telegram with his race number: 225.

. . . .

"Yonkers Marathon. Place: 1st. Time: 2 hr. 24 min. 25 seconds.
Comments: Very pleased with the above. Am now on the U.S.
team. Race went surprisingly well for me. In a group of four or so for
the first 10 miles. Took over about 10 miles and gradually increased the
pace. Did not seem to notice the heat much until about 15 miles. It
hit me quite rapidly after that. I was laboring quite a lot by 20 miles,
but managed to carry on and finished in good shape really considering
the heat. Took liquids very often during the race and a few vitamin c
pills. Had no internal difficulty. Figure my time might have been
worth about 10 minutes faster in cooler weather and on a faster course
(flatter)."

CHAPTER TWENTY

*"In the future everyone will
be famous for 15 minutes."*
Andy Warhol, 1968

The American sporting press which had ignored Buddy for four years discovered him in the rush of his Olympic trials victory, in the drama of high heat and collapsing runners, and hurried to cover the story of this strange expatriate American. Soon, through the pages of *Sports Illustrated* and *The Saturday Evening Post,* it was common knowledge that an American runner had been living in England, training as the English did at distances well over 100 miles per week, and that he had run faster than anyone ever had in the marathon, a long run of some kind that they ran in the Olympic Games. People also learned that the runner lived simply, ate sparingly, raced widely and— a point of some astonishment— drank beer occasionally.

For Buddy the attention was gratifying, but it did not bring even a pause to his training. The day after Yonkers he jogged 30 minutes and was on his way again. Two days after the Trials he flew home to Sioux Falls to thank his friends and to speak at a Chamber of Commerce luncheon in his honor. While there he ran with his friend Bill Erickson, safely home from his year in England, now landlocked and far away from sardines and Buddy's races, and he prepared to run a well-known

Flying high at the 1964 NAIA track meet.

regional road race, the 15.5-mile White to Brookings.

On May 29, Buddy ran 30 minutes steady before attempting his first hard workout since the Yonkers Marathon, 20 x 440. He completed the interval session in decent shape but found that his legs seemed to be pounding a lot. The next day he again ran easily in the morning before doing 5 x 1 mile with a full mile jog between each. On this run he noticed that "he felt tight in the hips for some reason." The date was May 30, 1964. Although Buddy didn't know it at the time, it was the first sign of the injury every athlete fears. It was the injury from which he would not recover.

. .

Buddy followed a high school boy in the early miles from White to Brookings before going off on his own. In high wind and 78 degree temperature he ran hard to win easily from his friend and former college teammate Ron Daws.

College sport is a time for exaggerated accomplishment and petty humiliation. When Edelen and Daws were in college together, Buddy was the accomplished athlete. Coach Jim Kelley a time or two even asked Ron to stop running intervals with Buddy for fear that he would trip him. By now, however, Ron Daws was finding his stride at distances that fit him. He was running long and gently and successfully. After he finished the Brookings race, he spoke with Buddy, who encouraged him to continue running, to move up to the marathon and to travel internationally for the experience. In four years, Daws himself, too slow and too dangerous to run with Edelen on the track at the University of Minnesota, would be on the United States Olympic team as a marathoner.

Meanwhile, at the White to Brookings race, the tightness in Buddy's hips escalated to pain. Thereafter, every run was affected by sharp pain first in the hips and then in the back. Buddy, it appeared, had placed himself squarely in a vice. All of America would be watching him closely during the Olympic Marathon because he had run so well at Yonkers, but that run had injured him. The combination of circumstances posed the question: now that Buddy had everyone's attention, what could he expect to do with it?

CHAPTER TWENTY-ONE

*"I gave every ounce of strength
I had right to the end."*

The Olympic Marathon in 1964 would be run on October 21. Abebe Bikila prepared for the event with a 2:16 time trial over the full 26 miles and 385 yard distance in August. He then had his appendix taken out on September 16 and who could credit his chances?

Buddy Edelen was America's great hope at this distance, certainly the finest prospect for the gold medal since Johnny Hayes picked up Dorando Pietri's leavings in 1908. But Buddy was injured and his preparation was uneven. Nevertheless the collected experts of *Track and Field News* in September 1964 selected Buddy as the favorite in this event which defies prediction. If nothing else, the prediction was a tribute to Buddy for what he had accomplished in the past and, for some, a hope and a prayer in his behalf.

Beyond these two lay Basil Heatley, who relieved Buddy of his world best in the Marathon by running 2:13:55 ahead of Ron Hill in the 1964 Poly; Japan's Kokichi Tsuburaya; Ethiopia's second string Mamo Wolde, an exceptional runner in his own right; Brian Kilby of England, the 1962 European champion; as well as the New Zealanders, Puckett, Keats and Julian. For special interest one could look to the track men moving up for a try at the long race. Ron Clarke and Tony Cook of Australia were entered as were Jim Hogan of Ireland and Bruce Kidd of Canada. Altogether it was a strong field with many potential winners and much room for disappointment.

For Buddy the period before the Olympic Marathon was turned upside down by his injury. While he would have expected in the midsummer of 1964 to put down his usual strong volume of quality running, mixing long runs at speed with quick interval work, his back made that impossible. Instead the midsummer months were static at best.

Buddy returned from America to England on June 8. Thereafter his days were painful and frustrating. On June 9, the first day back, his hips were still sore. On June 10, Buddy recorded in his diary that the hips were very stiff but seemed to improve as he got going on a set of 5 x 330; he also noticed, however, that his "rear end" was now affected. Increasingly the pain interfered with his training. On June 17, he planned an extended series of quarter mile repeats but quit after 10 of them, barely a warm-up in better days, saying that "on about the ninth one I felt a very sharp pain in the hip, so I quit at 10 and just ran home." On June 18, the pain "centered on the left leg...sore from the left hip on down the hamstring to the back of the knee on the left leg" and caused "considerable discomfort while running."

In desperation, Buddy finally tried rest. He did not run at all between June 22 and July 1, 1964. And still the pain continued. So Buddy resumed training but at much lower levels than at his peak. He ran shorter interval sessions, hoping to avoid the pounding of a hard road run, and he cut his Sunday run from the usual 22 to 11 miles, all that he could endure in the circumstance. On this training, he maintained his condition, perhaps, but no more and still the pain continued, joined now by a sharp pain in the shin on his left leg.

Finally on August 1, Buddy realized that the Games were too close for further delay and that, pain or no, he must train. The long runs returned as the anchor to his program, starting with a 14-mile run on Sunday, August 2, and then increasing immediately to the more customary 22-mile distance. He returned to a Wednesday long run, consistent with Fred's long stated advice that a marathoner must have two longish runs per week, and he approached his prior level and intensity of interval work.

Buddy wanted to stay and train in England until several days before the Olympic Marathon. It was a routine he had used success-fully in the past and one he trusted. But AAU officials refused his request and he was required to travel to Tokyo with the team, which meant first a long trip from England to California, a layover there and finally the flight to Tokyo en masse well before the marathon would have required his presence.

Nevertheless, by the time Buddy left England on this itiner-ary, September 9, he felt quite fit again despite the pain. In California for the layover he got in a run of 27 to 28 miles in 2:43. Upon his arrival in the Olympic Village he continued to lengthen the long run while maintaining speed and efficiency with shorter sessions, occasionally in the company of America's milers. On Sunday, October 4, Buddy ran 30 miles in 2:50 and on Sunday, October 11, he ran 50 to 52 kilometers in 2:52.

Just once he saw Bikila, who had started running again within 11 days of his operation. Face to face as they went different directions on a training run, Bikila moved to him and past without change of expression, so focused on the job at hand that he recognized nothing else. Buddy smiled to himself: Bikila, appendix in or appendix out, shoes on or shoes off, was disquieting indeed. Buddy ducked his head and ran on, harder still.

Getting ready now, Buddy trained alone and he trained with friends. Always he trained with the skepticism of his American team coaches, who feared "staleness" and "burn out" as if ignorant of the volume of work necessary for world-class marathoning. Even fellow American marathoner Pete McArdle, a hard worker himself, had at least some reservation about Buddy. After holding on through 25 miles of one 30-mile effort, said Pete, as he climbed into a trailing jeep, he's a madman, he is, but strong as a horse. He may at that have caught the essence of Buddy Edelen in 1964.

. .

Listen to the voices. An American distance runner in the early 1960s heard what Buddy heard. That the United States was a soft society dominated by soda swigging teen-agers, lounging contentedly by long, finned cars, each such teen-ager more apprehensive than the next of physical effort, outside the bashing of American football, which itself was something definitional.

Buddy addressed that opinion in English cross-country meets, on the continent in European affairs in which no other American had participated much less succeeded. He answered it in England's oldest and most traditional marathon, the Poly, and on the plains of Marathon itself. He answered as well behind the Iron Curtain and in the Orient and he did so always alone. In Tokyo, Buddy was determined to carry on as best he could. But he knew in his heart that his victory would be measured not by gold, silver or bronze, but by courage and perseverance. It was for others to drive home his message, that there was nothing inherent in America's nature that would prevent success at something hard, something that required planning and consistent effort and toughness.

Billy Mills was a Native American. More centrally, Billy Mills was a U. S. Marine with time to train in 1963 and 1964 and with sound advice moving him from heavy intervals to a program which emphasized long running and directed sharpening work. Most importantly in the final analysis, Billy Mills was a proud man who would not take no for an answer.

On the first day of track and field competition in Tokyo, Buddy watched Billy Mills run in the 10,000 meters with mounting astonishment. Mills with the world-record holder, Ron Clarke, Mills with Mohamed Gamoudi, even Mills with Mamo Wolde so far ahead of Ivanov and Tsuburaya, Halberg, Bolotnikov and Kidd, was not logical, not this deep into the event.

Buddy knew Billy Mills as a fellow South Dakotan. He had watched in the Village as Billy was ignored by even the shoe manufacturers, generally eager to put their product on any foot that twitched in

142

the Olympic Stadium. He had even discussed this race with Billy and
agreed, as a matter of courtesy and tact only, when Billy said: "I will
win." Now as Gamoudi shouldered his way between Clarke and Mills
on the last lap of a fast 10,000 meters, shoving Mills far to the outside
in the process, Buddy saw the look of anger and hurt and revenge
sweep Billy's features and from his seat he knew it had finally
happened: they had gone too far.

And when Mills found firm ground in the outside lanes and
used it for a one-punch gold-medal knockout of Gamoudi and Clarke,
Buddy—alone for so many years in his one room flat in England, alone
on the tracks and on the roads of Europe, alone with the derision other
countries felt for American distance running, crippled and frustrated,
fearful of his race and his chance to see it through, with his ambitions
and his years of sacrifice torn by injury—felt joy and satisfaction for his
friend Billy Mills. He carries that feeling with him to this day.

When Buddy later in the Games saw Bob Schul, a farmboy
from Ohio trained on the fast tracks in Los Angeles, win the 5,000 meters
and Bill Dellinger move past a disheartened Michel Jazy to pick up the
bronze medal, he knew the job was done or nearly so, the job he had
set for himself so many years ago. It was ironic really. Buddy had held
each insult to American distance running so close to his heart. And now
it was pay-back time and it was for others to do the job.

With a choice between tears and laughter at the turn of events,
Buddy did neither. He trained and he prepared himself to run, as Fred
had once said he could, to hell and back.

· · ·

Moods being what they are, even a normal person may
occasionally inflict pain on himself or herself, more as a curiosity than
to fulfill a need. Like most other sensations of which the body is
capable, pain has its satisfactions. Anticipated pain is quite another
thing, however. And it was anticipated pain that dogged Buddy's
thoughts as he prepared finally for the Olympic Marathon on the last
day of competition.

After a restless night, he awoke early on the day of the event. He satisfied himself with a light breakfast and returned quickly to his room for a solid job of pacing up and down the halls, waiting, fearful, apprehensive, just plain scared. Not with the matter of winning or losing. Absent a miracle, his back had answered that question. It hurt badly and, although he gave it some thought, ultimately Buddy decided not to use any pain killer. He considered cortisone but the English doctors warned that the drug would interfere with his adrenal gland. At the time, that seemed unwise. He left the drugs and kept the pain. Buddy's thoughts were of finishing, of running himself flat out as long and as hard as he could, to stay the course and to finish. Just finish.

He had a massage later in the morning of the event. Idling the morning away, he cut the colorful border off the bottom of his racing shorts, he hacked the arms off the team T-shirt, he located his kerchief and, satisfied at last that his uniform would be more comfortable than stylish, he went to the stadium. The day was dark and overcast, humid, as he and the others were led onto the immaculate red cinder track.

·   ·   ·   ·

It was 1 o'clock.

It was time.

In the middle of the pack of 68 runners Buddy took his place. On the inside, far off the back, was Bikila.

At the gun the field moved as one through the first 400 meters inside the stadium, led briefly by Yusaf of Pakistan and Kanda of Rhodesia before the big names arrived. Out the gate, into the tunnel and onto the course, Ron Clarke was up front; as were Jim Hogan, the Irishman in his first marathon; and Ron Hill. The Tunisian Hannachi was there as well, pressing an already fast pace well under five minutes for the first mile.

Clarke split 5,000 meters in 15:06 followed closely by Hogan in 15:08. Hill moved through in 15:14. In tow, Bikila drifted by in 15:19. Thereafter Bikila was content to follow Clarke through 10,000 meters in 30:14 and 15,000 meters in 45:35 before assuming control. By 20,000 meters Bikila was home free, moving past the marker in 1:00:58, only Hogan close in 1:01:3. For the others, this chase for the Olympic Gold Medal was history. And for Hogan it soon would be. To his credit, Jim Hogan tried to win. He held tight through the turn at halfway in 1:04:28 and he stayed on his feet through 35,000 meters. He could do no more and he did not finish this race.

Buddy Edelen thought the race would be won in 2:13: 48. It was just a guess, but he taped the splits for such a run to the inside palm of his left hand and set off with the gun. He hoped for some respite from his back and hips. He hoped for a gradually increasing pace, a marathon pace with a proper respect for the distance.

On this day, Buddy got nothing. The first five kilometers were sheer agony and it was made worse by the track men, screaming along up front and, as it happened, with no business in the event in the first place because they could not, or would not on this pace, last it.

What his back and the track men did was turn Buddy's marathon into a full-scale riot. For 26 miles, he ran through a deafening cordon of 500,000 Japanese, all feverishly interested in this event which they called "the flower." He hit every step hard, leaning backward slightly, torquing his arms this way and that, heedless of anything but the next step and, as the event progressed, the many runners out too fast coming back to him.

In the noise, it was hard to think; it was impossible to get a clear look at the race and see where he was. Although it wasn't true, Buddy had the impression that he was almost last as he turned at the pylon marking halfway. It didn't affect him for a moment. They were coming back now and he was running very hard indeed. He had hoped for a gradually increasing pace and had not gotten it. But now that he was adrift he would do what he could. He drove on through the crowd.

After a while, his legs got numb. He responded by trying to run faster. Nothing happened but he kept on pushing . . . pushing

The incomparable Abebe Bikila wins in Tokyo.

... pushing ... catching them one at a time now. He appeared for the first time among the leaders at 40,000 meters. It had taken him that long in an event which lasts 42,195 meters to assume his rightful position among the best marathoners in the world.

The last man Buddy Edelen passed before entering the Olympic Stadium to a cascading welcome was Aurele Vandendriessche, the winner of the 1963 Boston Marathon over Bikila. Buddy had no idea where he was in the field, but all the way around the track he continued to dig, his head tilting from side to side with pain and with fatigue; his lean straight back, and his fingers coiled tightly into fists, the nails cutting into the palms and drawing blood. In an event with a premium on relaxation this marathon had been run with the accelerator down all the way.

It did not bring Buddy a medal. It brought him sixth place and it brought him a final time of 2:18.12.4, some six minutes down on Bikila and almost four full minutes off his best. But it brought him quietude. He did what he could, absolutely everything he could. No one could have run harder.

Bikila ran 2:12:11, a new world best and an Olympic mark which would be there when Waldemar Cierpinski entered the stadium in Montreal in 1976. Basil Heatley of England ran a masterful race for second, letting the early fliers die in front of him, before outkicking Japan's Tsuburaya on the track. Basil ran 2:16:19.2; Tsuburaya got 2:16:22.8. In fourth and fifth came Kilby, also of England, in 2:17:02.4 and Jozef Suetoe of Hungary in 2:17:55.8.

· · · · ·

"Olympic Marathon," the diary notation said, "Place 6th-Time: 2:18:12. Pace felt terribly fast from the start. Drew out a schedule for 2:13:48 on my hand and found I was 30 seconds or so up on this at 10km. Legs became very tired and sore at 5-10 km. Began catching runners just before the turn—well back before—running very strongly last six miles but on guts alone."

"I could not have run a bit faster today after 20 km. A more moderate first 20 km may have meant a faster time; I don't know. Sciatica extremely painful. I'm not too disappointed. Feel I gave every ounce of strength I had right to the end."

· · · · · ·

The most important thing in the Olympic Games is not to win but to take part, just as in life the most important thing is not the triumph but the struggle. The essential thing is not to have conquered but to have fought well.

THE OLYMPIC CREED

CHAPTER TWENTY-TWO

"Couldn't have run today if I wanted to.
Had trouble walking."

The trouble in Tokyo was sciatica. It continued after Buddy left Japan, during his visits in Sioux Falls and in Lafayette and it continued even after his return to England. For a day or two at a time it might tease Buddy into thinking that it was better, but it would return the next day to flatten him. Day in and day out, Buddy ran with intense pain, each strike of the foot on hard ground a reminder of his new frailty.

The outward appearance of Buddy's schedule remained familiar in spite of the pain. He slowly moved the long run back over 20 miles, and as the winter gave way to early spring 1965, he went up to 28 miles. He still ran easy on Monday, something fast on Tuesday, something long on Wednesday, something short on Thursday and Friday. And he still loved to race. Even as his back dug at him, he accepted invitations to run several international cross-country races, at which he did surprisingly well all things considered, and he ran at home, most notably in the English national cross-country championships which had been, prior to Buddy's admission this year, closed to anyone unaffiliated with a commonwealth country. Finally, in late spring, he went cautiously back to the marathon.

The marathon was on May 2, 1965, in Kerfield, West Germany. Buddy won in 2:21 over undistinguished competition. At that, he let a German runner lead for 10 miles before reeling him back in over a course he found boring. The sciatica "became very sore about 10 miles and extremely sore and painful after the run."

That constant sciatic pain aside, the Kerfield Marathon at least gave Buddy a prospect for success in the major effort of this spring 1965. One more time, the Poly.

CHAPTER TWENTY-THREE

"I died a thousand deaths in this race."

Buddy was a resident in England for five years at the height of Pax Americana, a recognition that in the period after World War II it was America's natural place in world affairs to defend the free world and peace, even if it required waging war to do so. In a tradition-rich country like England, America's presumption must have been aggravating. Even allowing full credit for services rendered during the war, it surely would color an Englishman's attitude toward a visitor from the United States, Yanks as they were called. It would not have helped that the Americans withdrew Lend-Lease from Britain soon after World War II and that many people suffered personally as a result, nor would it have escaped notice that, when England's perceived interest in the Suez Canal was threatened, it was President Eisenhower who denied America's support and humiliated England in the international community.

None of this touched Buddy Edelen, although it could have, had he been a different sort. In fact, Buddy was too friendly, too accommodating, too sensitive to his environment to permit it. At a time when the phrase "ugly American" came to mean a peculiar blend of arrogance and ignorance, Edelen was openly patriotic, but not offensively so because he admitted the worth of other systems as well as his own. In fact, Buddy was in England to learn and he said as much. He particularly praised the English club system and credited it with maintaining a high standard of athletic competition throughout the country. Over time, that attitude, combined with his friendliness before and after competition, his willingness to turn out for small club affairs, his gameness in competition and his stride—that low, shuffling backward thing so easy for people to pick out in a crowd and so ungainly as to force a sense of identification with him—in time, all these things made Buddy one of the most popular runners in England. From being "a Yank" he became "the Yank" and finally, and certainly by 1963, he was "our Yank" to thousands of English people interested in athletics.

Never was the designation "our Yank" more appropriate than on June 22, 1965, when Buddy contested the Polytechnic Marathon for the third and last time. The field was highlighted by three Japanese runners, any one of whom could win. The favorite of the three, however, was Toru Terasawa, who had disappointed his countrymen by finishing 15th in Tokyo but rebounded to win at Beppu in 2:14:38. With Terasawa, the Japanese brought Morio Shigematsu, already the winner of the 1965 Boston Marathon in 2:16:33 while leading a 1-2-3-5-6 Japanese sweep, and Hirokazu Okabe, looking for vindication after running a miserable 31:00.6 in Tokyo's Olympic Games 10,000.

Against the Japanese, the English hoped to have Ron Hill, but he did not run, nor did Brian Kilby or Basil Heatley, Heatley having retired from competition. The only Englishman England had was Buddy Edelen, an American.

. .

The Polytechnic Marathon in 1965 was Buddy's last race in England. "I am going" he said, "with a great deal of mixed feelings. The welcome I have had over here, the friendships I have made, the experience I have gained are tremendous. All these people might call me an American ambassador in the sport. But I can assure you there has been a great deal of reciprocity in the five years I have been here."

For three years, Buddy had been trying to locate a photograph taken of him and the Queen of England in 1962, shortly before his run-in with the sardines. Now, as he approached the line for his last race, his last marathon, in England, the Polytechnic Harriers presented that prized photograph to him:

"I have chased that particular picture for three years. It was taken at my debut as a marathon runner in 1962 when Queen Elizabeth started the race at Windsor. The Polytechnic Harriers contrived to track it down. Their presentation of it to me as a farewell gift was a wonderful gesture I value and appreciate very much. That photograph goes to the top of my collection."

. . .

The 100 runners entered in the 1965 Polytechnic Marathon started at 2:50 p.m. from the stable on the Windsor Castle grounds. They ran between a brace of scarlet-dressed guards, turned left through a courtyard and then accelerated carefully down a hill to Windsor High Street. Past Eton College, under the M4, and they were on the way to Chiswick Stadium.

The Japanese forced the early pace. Ivor Edmunds, an optimistic Englishman, moved up occasionally to share the lead. Buddy stayed close and the five of them quickly moved away from the main pack. The pace was steady and fast but at 10 miles it was not fast enough for the three Japanese. They surged at Heath Lodge; then they surged again and again and again. Ivor Edmonds was gone early. Buddy stayed where he was, running in the triangle of Japanese: "I was flat out to stay with them. One or the other would start a burst and they gained 10 or 15 yards, and then I really had to move to catch them. I must have done it a dozen times and each time I was going as fast as if the finish was just a mile down the road." Buddy was joined as he ran by a crowd of British bicyclists. Every time the Japanese surged away from him the bikers would shout their encouragement, "C'mon Buddy! C'mon Buddy! Up, Buddy, Up!" and he would sprint.

Running with a triangle of Japanese.

Buddy held tight as long as he could but finally, even with the encouragement of his bicyclists, he had gone as far as he could go. He lost contact at 16 miles. From that point, he just kept his concentration and ran as fast as he could.

Shigematsu was unbeatable in this marathon. He started his drive for home shortly before the 20-mile mark, strangled his friend Terasawa with the quickened tempo and won by 500 yards in 2:12 flat, 11 seconds faster than Bikila had run at Tokyo. Terasawa finished next, in 2:13:41. For his persistence, Buddy had the pleasure of sneaking past the third Japanese, Okabe, thus preventing the sweep.

Buddy's time was 2:14:34, only six seconds slower than he ran as a world best in 1963. When he crossed the line in Chiswick Stadium, the five years that started on a boat ride from Finland in 1960 ended. As one newspaper article commented, "the greatest (contribution) from America since lease-lend has run his last marathon in England."

. . . . .

"Windsor to Chiswick (Poly) Marathon.
Place: 3rd. Time: 2 hrs.14 minutes and 34 seconds.

"Comments: Ivor Edmunds led the first part of the race with the
Japanese taking over from time to time. After five miles (25 minutes!),
we broke off into a group of five (three Japanese, Edmunds and I). I
felt very good through seven miles. No pain from sciatica, but it came
on about eight as the pace stiffened. Edmunds dropped back at 10
miles and I attempted to hang on. They put in terrific bursts and by 15
miles I was actually sprinting to keep with them. They dropped me
over a dozen times but I managed to work my way back up each time
by sprinting as though the finish was a mile or less down the road. I
dropped at about 16 miles.

"The sciatica was sheer hell the last six miles. Time was
amazing considering that I did not expect to crack 2:18. Shigematsu
won in 2 hr. 12 min. (world best). I managed to catch Kobe and pass
him for third the last two miles. Terasawa was second in 2:13. I died
a thousand deaths in this race especially from 10 to 15 miles. We were
about 1:15 at the 15-mile point! I cannot help but feel the sciatica made
some difference between 10-16 miles."

CHAPTER TWENTY-FOUR

*"30 minutes run on the roads. Started slowly
and gradually worked into it."*

Southeast Essex would be different after Buddy's last run in England on July 27, 1965. For five years the neighborhood had set its clock by Buddy's morning run, his evening return, his trot down the street for a paper and the tidbits of food he called dinner, his back-and-forth jaunts along the sea front. People grew accustomed to his haphazard dress, the bizarre collection of torn sweat shirts strangely lettered, his dark socks stuck into old shoes, the backward lean as he ran and the twisted arm; through it all, the friendly word and the smile, always the acknowledgement that he was a guest in their country.

The streets would be quiet, like those rare days without a breeze off the sea front, just enough to make a person pause, notice the stillness and then move on.

. .

Dear Jimmy,

I would like to request a few lines to express, through the medium of the *Athletics Weekly* magazine, my appreciation and gratitude to all the athletes, officials, and friends I have had the pleasure of becoming acquainted with since 1960.

The opportunity of living in England has not only enabled me to develop into an international distance runner, it has afforded me the chance of making many close friendships which I shall cherish for many years to come.

I know my coach, Fred Wilt, would like me to convey his gratitude as well, since it was at Fred's suggestion that I first decided to come to England.

The experience I gained through four years of active participation in British athletics contributed immeasurably in helping me to represent the U.S.A. in the Tokyo Olympics and for this alone I feel indebted.

I shall be returning to the U.S.A. to begin work on my master's degree in Colorado, and I must admit that it is with considerable reluctance than I shall be leaving.

I would like to convey a special thanks to the officials of the B.A.A.B. and the E.C.C.U. for their kind cooperation and help; to Mel Watman, Sam Ferris and others on the *Athletics Weekly* staff who have given such generous coverage to my performances over the road, track and country; to the athletes and officials at the two clubs I have been affiliated with, Chelmsford and Hadleigh; and finally to the many other athletes and friends I have made over the past five years.

Thank you all very much.

Yours Sincerely,

"Buddy" Edelen

Editor's response: "I know that the many friends Buddy refers to will wish me to say how much we have enjoyed the company and friendship of the finest ambassador this country has ever had from the U.S.A. We shall always remember you with affection and hope to see you back again one day."

. . .

On July 28, 1965, Buddy Edelen left England for New York. He had finished what he started. He had proved that an American could carry his part of the deal in club events too numerous to count; that an American could handle the mud, the fences, the undulations of English cross country; that an American could hold his own in the pushing and shoving of international cross country. He had proved that an American could persevere through mind-numbing times and distances on the track against the best Britain had to offer; and he had proved, finally, that in the longest and most quizzical event of all, the marathon, an American could not only compete but excel. The list of the ten fastest marathons ever run was testament to his accomplishment:

1. Morio Shigematsu, Japan: 2:12:00
2. Abebe Bikila, Ethiopia: 2:12:11
3. Toru Terasawa, Japan: 2:13:41
4. Basil Heatley, England: 2:13:55
5. Ron Hill, England: 2:14:12
6. Buddy Edelen, United States: 2:14:28
7. Buddy Edelen, United States: 2:14:34
8. Toru Terasawa, Japan: 2:14:38
9. Brian Kilby, England: 2:14:43
10. Toru Terasawa, Japan: 2:14:48

Years ago, under the bleachers at Purdue University, Fred Wilt told Buddy Edelen that he could be an Olympian. Leaving England, he was that much and more.

Arriving in New York he was alone and forgotten. Buddy's 15 minutes were over. He spent a solitary day in the city and then went home to Sioux Falls for a visit of several weeks, during the middle of which he made a long drive to Lafayette, Indiana. With Fred, Buddy finalized the plans for the fall. Buddy would enter Adams State College in Alamosa, Colorado, for joint purposes. He would accept a graduate assistant job and study for his master's degree in psychology. He would also, at the 7,540-foot altitude of Alamosa, prepare for the 1968 Olympic Games, which would be held in Mexico City's comparable rarefied air.

Buddy drove from Sioux Falls, South Dakota, to Alamosa, Colorado, on September 8 and 9, 1965. He settled into teaching, for which he received the modest compensation of $150 per month. He bagged groceries for extra income. And he ran, haunted by a prospect more uncertain each day. As he says now, "deep down, I had this horrible feeling that my career was over. I've often felt that distance runners, especially those who have been running for some 10 years or more, are probably better in tune with their injuries than most physicians. Even back then I somehow knew that my condition was degenerative; that once it had come on, running 130-150 miles a week on it was not going to make it go away. In a way, as the weeks and months passed I felt like a terminal cancer patient, hoping beyond all hope for a miracle cure. The psychological conflict was terrible. On the one hand, I knew that I had the perseverance, dedication, singularity of purpose and tenacity to make it happen. On the other, I knew I had absolutely no control of what had happened or what was to happen to my sciatica. So I just kept plugging along, hoping for something."

CHAPTER TWENTY-FIVE

*"The human body simply cannot be expected to perform
with the same efficiency at 7,540 feet as it does at sea level.
The past month has proven that to me."*

The picture of Buddy Edelen in Alamosa is memorized by a generation of runners. He is alone, heavily hooded, grey, lurching past a sign that shows the force against which he struggles: 7,540 feet. That altitude cramped him, caused his nose to bleed, short-circuited his long run, slowed his interval runs, killed his racing, promised no reward and still there he was. He was running. He was running, in part, because he always had. He had run at Sioux Falls in high school, at the University of Minnesota, briefly in San Francisco before the trials in 1960, in Finland, finally in England and from there all over the world. He had accepted that he was slow and he made himself as fast as he could be and as strong as no others. He had surged when he felt fatigue; burned when he felt insulted; felt the sting of the Japanese and the many bursts and the bicyclists' discontent. He had run with pain in his hip and in his back, tracing through the hamstrings to his knees and buckling him. And in all, Buddy Edelen—because of it, because of the pain, and the travel, the relative poverty that came from maintaining only a job that permitted training and travel, because of his obscurity and his bent frame—defined running for his period.

The force against which he struggles.

From all outward manifestations, running was sacrifice. Distracted by that reality, only a very few people ran anyway and for them the sacrifice proved illusory. As it happened, the process itself, the continuity of running every day, had its own rewards, more valuable than money and, in some ways, incompatible with having it. A runner's life was meant to be lean and hard and the satisfactions were meant to come from within.

When running was like that, athletics was inquiring and elemental; it posed questions about the human spirit that were beyond how far, how long, by what mechanical process. When Buddy, for example, slogged through 135 miles a week in a hard English winter, or when he sprinted to maintain contact with the Ethiopians in Athens or the Japanese in London, when he drove himself over the course in Tokyo despite his bad back, the question was not so much how he did that but why he did that.

Because the question rarely resolved itself in material terms, running was pointless to many people. Others, far more fortunate, recognized intuitively that the very pointlessness of running was its greatest strength. That pointlessness meant that no spectator could ever entirely know what was going on as he watched a distance being run. The casual spectator might have a single clue: he had what he saw. The better informed spectator might have additional clues, by knowing what performances had been rendered in the past by the particular athlete. Finally, the best informed spectator, the one most likely to understand what he saw, would know something of the athlete's background, what made him the way he was, what made him compete when competition was meaningless, when at the end of the day he would have a clap on the back and perhaps a cheap cup. With that level of interest and understanding, a spectator, surely at this point more amateur sleuth and psychiatrist, could place the performance in context and approximate understanding. In sum, when running was pointless, running was fascinating because running had very little to do with running. It had to do with people and why they act the way they do.

With money in the sport, athletics is diminished. Can anyone question why a person runs fast when that person makes hundreds of thousands of dollars if he or she does? Is there uncertainty in his purpose? Is there any interest in an event which, fundamentally, is no different from any other competitive mercantile proposition? Not coincidentally, as money has come to the sport, so have the cheaters, drug addicts and growth hormone freaks who rob the event not only of interest but of certainty. With this kind of taint, even the mechanical achievement of running a few tenths of a second faster, or throwing a shot a centimeter more, is uninteresting because now that the motivation is clear—money— achievement is not. No advance is without suspicion that the athlete cheated in a way as yet undetectable. Far better, the old days when accomplishment was clear and motivation was not.

Those better days of athletic accomplishment were epitomized by John Landy of Australia. When misunderstanding people chased him in 1954 as he chased the first four-minute mile, Landy pointed out that his stride was as it had been, only a stride or two farther up the track this year than last. So what was all the hubbub?

. . .

Buddy ran fast before there was any money in it. The most he ever made from a single event was $500. While that amount was more than his monthly teaching salary and not insignificant, Buddy never got rich off the sport and his motivations were anything but financial. His motivations therefore are fair game. Why would a runner do the things that Buddy did when others, similarly situated, did not?

To some extent, Buddy was just plain lucky. Without Fred Wilt, Buddy might have been another gifted collegian who stopped running upon graduation. Fred intervened; he provided opportunity in Finland first and then in England that made it possible for Buddy to continue with his running.

Even at that, however, there must be an additional explanation, because Fred did not exactly set Buddy up in a comfortable berth. To understand why Buddy would take the opportunity to flay himself for five years in England with a low paying teaching job, while his contemporaries were settling down to career, wife and children, it is good to know him before he ran.

Leonard Edelen was born on September 22, 1937, in Harrodsburg, Kentucky. His mother was hospitalized when he was 6 and he did not see her again until he was an adult. Because his father travelled, Buddy spent some months after the institutionalization of his mother with an aunt in Alabama and, later, at a Roman Catholic boarding school. Impressionable and suggestible, he thought seriously at boarding school of becoming a priest, undeterred by the fact that he wasn't even Catholic. In the meantime, his father married and remarried. On the third marriage Buddy was returned to the family home, where, however, he saw his father only infrequently during the week. While Buddy maintains that his father "always gave more than he took" and was a generous man, the fact is that on weekends his father occasionally drank to excess, according to the son, and was verbally abusive.

By the time Buddy entered middle or junior high school, he

163

Buddy Edelen as a high school senior, back row, third from left.

had flirted with delinquency, even going so far as to participate in a heist of merchandise from the home of a local FBI man, who took a predictably dim view of the event when he learned of it. Buddy also ballooned from physical inactivity and a natural propensity to gain weight. Only 5 feet 6 inches tall as he entered high school, by now in Minneapolis, Minnesota, with his father, he weighed 155 pounds and carried the colorfully descriptive name of "Butterball Bud."

As a means of activating her stepson, Mrs. Edelen encouraged Buddy to try a sport at St. Louis Park High School. He considered football his sophomore year but was sidetracked by a hernia. Finally, in his junior year he tried out for the cross-country team. He was an immediate success as a runner, struck by the feeling that he could "jog forever without getting tired," and very early he decided that he had discovered something that could change his life forever. On his own, with the knowledge and approval of his first high school coach, Roy Griak, later appointed head track coach at the University of

164

Minnesota, Buddy ran several miles each morning before joining the team workouts in the afternoon. The extra workouts, together with his natural strength, made him the best runner at St. Louis Park. He won races as an incident of his main goal, which was to "finish a race feeling as though I could not possibly have run another second faster." With success as a runner, Buddy was transformed. His confidence improved, his weight dropped, he became a social performer rather than the loner he had been once. He established his new identity. He was a runner.

That identity separated Buddy from others in the school and he thereafter worked hard to maintain it. Paradoxically, as he accepted running as his self-definition, he mistrusted his ability. Even in high school, at a time when his basic speed was at least average and maybe a little better than that, he felt that he could not run fast so he must run long. He trained harder with that in mind.

When Buddy's father took a new job in Sioux Falls, South Dakota, Buddy moved there with him for his senior year in high school. He immediately rewrote the record book in every meet. He ended the year as South Dakota state champion in cross-country and track, and undefeated. His streak and his accomplishments were the product of consistent running, in excess of what was asked of him. Bill Erickson, who was a high school teammate before joining Buddy at the University of Minnesota (and later in England), remembers that if the high school coach assigned four quarter-mile repeats, Buddy was likely to do eight. He also continued to run in the morning.

Upon graduation, Buddy accepted a partial athletic scholarship at the University of Minnesota, where again he was immediately successful because of his natural strength and his tendency to train more than requested. He also benefitted at the University from the coaching of Jim Kelley, who wisely let Buddy design most of his own workouts: coaching by acquiescence. Coach Kelley knew that Buddy would do what was required and that he was smart enough to do it right.

In the years before Buddy met Fred Wilt, the pattern is one in which an insecure athlete finds a sense of identity in the sport and maintains that identity only by succeeding. It is also one in which the athlete mistrusts his own ability and "compensates" by working hard. There is also to Buddy's training and racing an element of self-fulfilling prophecy or something close to it. Buddy created an impression of himself as the kind of person who could and would accept any discomfort in order to run well. He then raced to that idealized self- concept. His coaches, Fred Wilt included, noted the characteristic and encouraged it. On one occasion in 1960, Fred wrote: "Remember, Buddy, I have always told you that you are rougher than a cob when it comes to running, and you are getting rougher all the time. You can be defeated, but a man is damn well going to feel like he has been run backward through a hammer mill if he does take you. You have the background, experience, confidence and just plain guts now to kick hell out of almost anybody if you get half a chance. You can make it just as hard or just as easy as you like on the opposition. Each race takes you to the grave and back but you can do it." Buddy accepted this kind of talk, internalized it, and raced and trained in conformity, or to conform, with it.

It was, then, a combination of insecurity and self-concept that drove Buddy to train and race as he did. Ironically, it was this same combination that also caused the one continual conflict between Buddy and Fred. Buddy would not rest no matter how strongly Fred encouraged it until injury or exhaustion required it. If Buddy rested before a race, he could feel his condition draining out of him, so he was inclined to train right up to the important races and then, only at the last minute, stop and take a day or two of total rest. Buddy virtually never "tapered" toward an event by reducing volume and intensity gradually. Fred knew what he was up against and he tried regularly to get Buddy to understand himself well enough to change: "the compulsion to run and restlessness comes from mental inferiority complex"; "here comes the old insecurity again"; "you are just now to the point where you could go too far"; "I cannot kill your spirit but you are your own worst enemy. Why not be kind to Buddy Edelen? Why kill him now?" Fred's protests illustrate the sharp edge in Buddy Edelen. The same motivations that made Buddy a good runner could also destroy him.

Buddy Edelen, 1966.

In considering motivation, however, it is too simple to identify insecurity and say there it is, for what accomplishment cannot be
explained and demeaned in such manner. There must be more
because, after all, the world is full of insecure people, but it is
relatively shy of accomplishment. The "something more" in athletics
can be found in "types" illustrated by Paavo Nurmi and Emil Zatopek.

All runners are familiar with the imagery of Paavo Nurmi.
Stern, unrelenting, to a certain extent ungenerous and manipulative
but, finally, scientific and experimental, Paavo Nurmi was better than
the runners he found on the track with him because he outthought
them before he outran them. From a distance of more than 50 years
and an almost unsurmounted language barrier, Paavo Nurmi is rec-
ognizably a scientific man applying methods to practice.

Emil Zatopek could also be described as scientific, at least to
the extent that he, like Nurmi, used his body as a laboratory. But Emil
Zatopek was more than that, and to explain his success as a runner you
go beyond mere advances in training. Emil Zatopek enjoyed running
and he enjoyed the people with whom he ran. Who can forget the story
of Zatopek toying with his 5,000-meter qualifying heat in Helsinki,
trying earnestly to slow the pace by assuring his friends that they all,
late in the trial, were safe and would surely qualify? Or Zatopek asking
Peters whether the pace was acceptable in the marathon and, upon
hearing that it was too slow, shrugging his shoulders and going faster?
Or Zatopek carrying his wife through the snow as a means of increasing
the difficulty and therefore the worth of his workout?

The point to all this, in addition to verifying the extent to
which distance running is susceptible to interpretation as well as
measurement, is that there may be at least three and probably many
more "types" of successful long-distance runner: 1. the insecure person who finds reassurance in the hard grind of distance running; 2. the
scientific person who tinkers with his body and for whom the running
itself may well be incidental; and 3. the person who runs from the pure
joy of it. This list of three does not even approach a fourth potential,
that of a person who is truly self-loathing and runs to punish himself
and the more the better, because that kind of motivation is ultimately

so distasteful and self-defeating as to bear no conversation.

Of the primary three motivations described above (omitting the fourth), Buddy would qualify for each. The insecurity has been discussed. As to the scientific, it must be remembered that while Fred set the broad contour of Buddy's training, Buddy did the fine tuning himself. He planned the specific workouts. His diary shows that he knew exactly where he was supposed to end up, physically, and that he enjoyed the constant adjustment of his program to meet that end. It is also evident, although he sometimes denied it, that Buddy enjoyed the physical act of running and that he was as amiable in his relations as Emil had been. There would be no other way to explain the notably friendly relationship Buddy had with the running community in England. They shared his joy.

As Buddy ran, however, through the fall of 1965 and into the winter of 1966 in the high altitude of Alamosa, that joy had become an increasingly distant memory. The altitude was bad enough but it was the back that made things unbearable. Buddy had been running in pain now for more than a year and was going on two. The sharp edge in Buddy Edelen was beginning to cut.

CHAPTER TWENTY-SIX

"As the thread outlasts the spool,
so the thorn, the rose."

John Hollander

One year and one month after running 2:14 at the Polytechnic Buddy ran and won the Denver Marathon. Even accounting
for altitude the time was a shock. It was 2:51 and Buddy had some
trouble running down a teen-ager from New Mexico, who had a four
minute lead on him at the 15-mile mark. The win, no matter the
time, might have been hopeful for a younger runner coming through;
for a runner of Buddy's accomplishment it was a last gasp.

He did not resign from his sport as a professional ballplayer
would and have his salary cease while he sought or was forced to
seek more productive work. Rather, he kept running and for some
time even maintained the habits of competition, including the
scrupulous record. But the record was unkind, full of back pain, bad
hamstrings, slow runs and cortisone shots. At a time when it was
difficult for him even to get out of bed in the morning, it was natural
that he would turn to other things, and he did. Buddy increasingly
invested more of his energy in projects for the college than for
himself and his running.

He worked hard with Joe Vigil, the track coach of Adams

Ken Moore, George Young, and Ron Daws,
United States Olympic team members, 1968 marathon.

State, to bring the Olympic Trials Marathon in 1968 to Alamosa. When he and Joe succeeded and the event was held, the other runners did not believe until the gun went off that Buddy would not, at the last minute, line up and give it a shot. But he did not.

He stood on the sidelines on August 18, 1968, a spectator along with the 3,000 other people he had persuaded to line the course and provide encouragement. He watched with them, with strangers to his ambition, the 129 Olympic hopefuls begin the first of five 5.2-mile loops, watched the early pacesetters fade into high altitude and extravagant expectation, watched Ken Moore of Oregon assume the lead at 10.4 miles in 57:38, and watched George Young of Arizona finally make the decisive move in the last miles, for a winning time of 2:30:48, with Moore second. He also watched Ron Daws survive a last-minute surge by Bob Deines, an early practitioner of something called "long, slow distance," and hold the

171

precious final spot on the United States Olympic team.

Billy Mills was in Alamosa for that 1968 Olympic Trials Marathon. In an attempt to make his second Olympic team, Mills ran as far as his own bad back would permit and then he stopped. At the time, Billy Mills said only that he would retire, that "today" would be the first day of the rest of his life. For him, however, there was an Olympic Gold medal, and with it, the sure knowledge that he was secure, if not materially then at least in the memory of many. Buddy Edelen had no such comfort.

Early in his marathon career, he considered that he would mature with the event, that he would get stronger with age, be better in 1968 than in 1964 and at least potentially better in 1972 than in 1968. He even wagered a friend in 1965 that he would run 2:30 when he was 60. As it happened, the marathon crippled him before he could test his theory. Standing on the sidelines in Alamosa, the hopes were gone. Only the pain remained.

CHAPTER TWENTY-SEVEN

"He's an impostor, Frank!"

Erich Segal

When Frank Shorter coasted into the Olympic Stadium in 1972, behind only an impostor in shorts given full access to the track for a single interesting lap, it was tempting to put Buddy up as his predecessor, a part of his natural lineage, as a means of bringing some glory to Buddy for accomplishments not fully recognized in his own country. In fact, Frank Shorter's Olympic Gold Medal in Munich was no part of Buddy Edelen. If heritage is sought for Shorter, it is the heritage of Gainesville, the Florida Track Club and Jack Bachelor.

Buddy Edelen can stand on his own. When Buddy went to England in 1960 most Europeans laughed openly at American distance runners. Buddy stopped that laughter. He replaced it with friendship and respect, for himself and for his country.

That is Buddy Edelen's story.

AFTERWORD

Buddy Edelen remained on the staff at Adams State College until 1980. He resigned at that time and eventually relocated to Tulsa, Oklahoma. In the interim, he finished his master's degree in psychology, built a reputation as one of the more popular teachers on campus, went a long way toward a Ph.D. and almost died in 1971 when his Volkswagen was hit by an International Scout with a railroad tie for a bumper. The impact broke his pelvis in three places, most of his ribs, his shoulder, his clavicle and made a hole in his diaphragm. It is characteristic of Buddy that, as he recovered from the accident, he found the good in it. For a time, he maintained that the impact had shifted his spine in such a way that the pressure on his sciatic nerve was reduced. That wasn't entirely true and even at the date of this writing his back hurts. Of course, he doesn't help things by running every day, which he does.

From and since his resignation from Adams State he has had good moments and bad, but not essentially different from those of us who have not run world bests and circled the Olympic Stadium. Today it is hard to see the young Buddy Edelen in his face until you get him into conversation. That quickly brings him out in the open, indomitable, cheerful, full of blarney, imbued with a trust that everything will turn out well.

He tells, in the manner of all good runners, at least one lie repetitively, always carefully identifying it as such. He claims that years ago he gave an interview in Europe shortly before flying back to the United States. As he tells it the interviewer forgot to ask him how old he was and wired the following inquiry: "How old Buddy?" To which Edelen responded, "Old Buddy fine. How you?"

The story is from somebody else's life. But it fits Buddy just right.

Buddy Edelen today.

Postscript

Buddy Who?

By Hal Higdon
Senior Writer, *Runner's World*

At a race in Tulsa, Oklahoma, Rod Dixon won over a field of several thousand runners. Afterwards, one of the race officials congratulated Dixon, introducing himself: "My name is Buddy Edelen." Dixon looked quizzically at the man: "Buddy Who?"

Buddy Edelen chuckled when he told me that story. I was in Tulsa visiting my old friend, researching an article about him that appeared in *The Runner,* August, 1982. Buddy was more bemused than angry that—despite being America's best marathoner during the years between Clarence DeMar and Frank Shorter— he was virtually unknown to the runners in the race that day. Later, he sent me a letter signed, "Buddy Who?"

That letter reminded me of the many letters I received from Buddy when he was in England during the early 60s, carefully typed on tissue-thin paper that folded into an air-mail envelope, called an Aerogramme. He never signed himself with his given name, Leonard Graves Edelen. It was always "Buddy," and always in quotes. Along with Fred Wilt, I was one of Buddy's links to the home he had left to become a great runner.

He certainly succeeded. Few marathoners from any country can match Buddy Edelen's record. Between 1962 and 1966, Buddy ran 13 marathons against top international competition and won seven of them, never placing worse than ninth. He defeated the best and broke their course records. He held eight American track records and won the British AAA 10-mile title with 48:31.4, fourth fastest ever. His 2:14:28 victory in the 1963 Polytechnic Marathon established a world best—and since 1925 he is the only American besides Alberto Salazar credited with having held the marathon world record. At the 1964 Olympic Trials in Yonkers, New York, he ran an incredible 2:24:26 in 91-degree heat , winning by more than 20 minutes in a race where 71 percent of the field—including me— quit. If Frank Shorter and Bill Rodgers do not stand in Buddy Edelen's shadow, they at least trod in his footsteps.

Let me offer another anecdote offered by Buddy during my 1982 visit to Tulsa. Before the start of an indoor two-mile race two decades earlier in New York, John Macy, a Polish defector, attempted to psych Buddy, sitting in the infield: "Minnesota boy, you no good!"

As Frank Murphy points out in this book, one thing that inflamed Buddy was the suggestion that European runners, particularly Iron Curtain ones, were superior to Americans. He snapped: "With six laps to go, look over your shoulder, Macy. I'll be coming past!"

With 14 laps gone in the 22-lap race, Edelen trailed only the Pole: "Two to go, Macy!" Next lap: "One more, Macy!" Finally: "Good-bye, Macy!" Buddy rushed past to victory.

Buddy related that story with a mixture of pride and embarrassment: "I'm not sure what got into me. I used to hate talking in the middle of a race. I felt it affected my concentration."

He felt he ran not merely for Buddy Edelen, but for all American distance runners, present and future. "It was a crusade. I wanted to prove Americans could run distance. I gave them a taste of it, and Frank Shorter finished them off."

Edelen was an iconoclast. At a time when taking liquids during a race was considered almost a sign of weakness, Buddy carried squeeze bottles in long workouts to practice drinking. When his English training companions chided him, saying it was not warm enough for water, he would reply: "Not today, but some day it will be."

He also drank other liquids. Reporters delighted in mentioning his affinity for Guinness stout (which Buddy defended by saying it also was good for nursing mothers). For a 1964 profile story on Buddy, *Sports Illustrated* published a photo of him hoisting a glass of stout in a pub. So before the Olympics that year, Buddy had no difficulty convincing Guinness to ship several cases to Tokyo.

American officials, however, were aghast when the cases arrived at the Olympic Village. They summoned Buddy to the team office. Buddy pleaded it was important he maintain his routine, but team officials considered stout in his room improper. "We finally compromised," recalls Buddy. "I kept my stout, but had to come down to the office to drink it."

As an occasional contributor to *Sports Illustrated*, I had provided some of the research for the 1964 article, calling upon memories of a trip the previous fall to Czechoslovakia for the Kosice Marathon. Buddy, of course, had won handily. I led the trail pack for a while, then failed badly in the closing miles, finishing in pain and despair while The Star-Spangled Banner was being played in his honor during the awards ceremony.

On the train back to Prague, Buddy astounded me by lighting a cigarette. Afterwards, I suspected he was doing it mainly for shock value. Bill Erickson, his Minnesota teammate who lived with him in England, claimed: "His beer-drinking reputation was exaggerated. You can't train hard with a hangover. Actually, it was pretty dull rooming with Buddy. He was always in bed by 10."

Frankly, I wasn't sure I wanted to read this book. Two of Buddy's best races—Kosice in 1963, Yonkers in 1964—had been among my worst. I felt it might be too painful to relive those moments.

So when Buddy asked me to write a few words, I thought I would skim quickly through the manuscript to remind me of the facts from a quarter century ago. That would be aid enough, I suspected, for the writing of an acceptable introduction—or, as it now turns out, a post-script. I would fulfill a self-imposed obligation to an old friend.

But, almost against my will, I found myself being drawn into the narrative as presented by Frank Murphy, a man I have never met, only spoken with on the telephone, a public administrator of all things, not a professional journalist. But, hats off, Frank. You did your job. I couldn't put the manuscript down. Perhaps I was confronting my own inadequacies as an athlete. But more than that, I feel that Frank has succeeded in capturing the spirit and innocence of those days before running became a professional sport.

I tried to recall my first encounter with Buddy. We lived in close proximity for several years without meeting. Buddy was still in high school in the Twin Cities while I was attending Carleton College in Northfield, Minnesota. I graduated in 1953; he enrolled at the University of Minnesota in 1955. I probably first read of his collegiate successes in *Track and Field News,* a publication I devoured from cover to cover back then. We were competing in different arenas; we never raced or met before 1959, to the best of my knowledge.

An artist as well as writer during my early career, I did the illustrations for Fred Wilt's book published in that year, *How They Train.* Buddy was one of the athletes whose portrait I drew from a photograph. It's a decent illustration of Buddy in a U of M sweat shirt, but looks nothing like him. I still have Fred's book, a classic for runners seeking training tips in the era before *Runner's World.* Somewhere in the attic, I must still have a photo of me racing in a pair of Golden Gophers team shorts that came into my possession after a stay by Buddy at my apartment in December 1959.

Neither Buddy nor I can remember whether he left them or I stole them. When I told Buddy about the shorts recently, he said he was initiating litigation; I reminded him of the statute of limitations. Money was in short supply for both of us back then. He probably offered the shorts as one might offer a bottle of wine when visiting a friend. Perhaps I felt that in keeping the shorts, I had captured Buddy's spirit, that I might draw energy from them, make me a better runner, him a lesser one. It didn't happen that way; only hard training works.

Buddy ran his first road race during that visit, returning from a stay with Fred Wilt in Lafayette. Fred, ever protective, undoubtedly arranged for the cheap room with me in Chicago. Buddy won the two mile in the Holiday Meet sponsored by the University of Chicago Track Club, for which I competed. I finished fourth. Seeking revenge, I lured him into a 10-mile race on the lake front the next morning, the Holiday Ten.

Also in that race was UCTC member Gar Williams, who coincidentally would win the National AAU Marathon in Yonkers in 1965, the year after Buddy's great victory. Details of the 10-mile have long faded from memory. It's a one-line entry on an old calendar page in my files. Gar recalls the race as being run in atrocious weather, eventually coming down to a kicking dual in the last quarter. I had the best kick and won in 48:51.9, which sounds impressive until you realize that nobody measured courses with any great accuracy back then. Gar finished second, Buddy third. We probably earned medals. Nobody offered appearance fees back then; accepting prize money was unheard of. I can only speculate at what it would cost for a race promoter to corral three runners of that caliber today.

Not only was that Buddy's first road race, it was the farthest he ever had run even in a workout! "That race served as a stimulus for me," he recalls. "It let me know that I was destined for distances longer than 2 miles."

Some stimulus. Few Americans within the next few years would get close enough to Buddy in a road race to have a chance at outkicking him. Certainly not me again.

Soon afterwards Buddy left for England. It was a move that I had considered for myself several years earlier. I had been stationed with the U.S. Army in Germany for 19 months, a period when I made tremendous strides as a runner. I considered moving to England to work and run. Love and marriage got in the way. I'm happy I stayed home, because I doubt returning to Europe would have made me a better runner, but the move was right for Buddy. In one sense, when Buddy headed for England in 1961, he was living one of my early dreams.

We continued to correspond. We also shared the same coach,

185

Fred Wilt. Buddy's stay in England contributed to his success, but it also resulted in his anonymity today. Earning $150 a month, he had no funds to return to the U.S. to compete in the one race that would have assured his lasting fame among Americans, the Boston Marathon. "Jock Semple wrote and begged me to run Boston," Buddy recalls, "but he had no money and I had no money."

Had Buddy heeded Jock's pleas at the peak of his career, he certainly could have won Boston two or more times. Belgium's Aurele Vandendriessche won in 1963 and 1964. Buddy beat the Belgian often in European races. I led Boston in 1964 until passed by Vandendriessche on the second of the four Newton hills, around 18 miles. I'm convinced Buddy would have dusted Vandendriessche on both occasions.

Bill Erickson says: "I told Buddy in 1962 that he should go back to Boston. That's where you got publicity in the United States. Winning the Poly, or Kosice, meant a lot in Europe, but few people back home heard of him." Pride was involved: why would Buddy want to pay to run Boston when other race organizers all over the world eagerly sought him?

I'm also convinced he would at least have medaled at the Olympic Games in Tokyo were it not for the stupidity of those who scheduled the Olympic Trials in Yonkers on a hot afternoon. I don't think anybody would have beaten Bikila, but Buddy was a frequent victor over Heatley, the silver medalist.

Let me tell you how bad it was at Yonkers. I was running with Buddy at 10 miles, but he soon pulled away and Norm Higgins moved into second while Johnny Kelley and I struggled behind. Given the weather, and despite Buddy's mammoth lead, it remained anybody's race. At 17 miles, I tried to pick up the pace to catch Higgins.

I started to hear ringing in my ears. I slowed; the ringing stopped. I picked up the pace again; the ringing resumed. This happened several times as my mind fought to overcome my body. It soon became clear to me that I had two choices: drop out or die!

Higgins came close to doing just that, remaining a week in the hospital after collapsing at 23 miles. Kelley persevered to finish 20 minutes back, third in a race he had won the eight previous years. Only

Buddy maintained anywhere near a reasonable pace. It was because of his tremendous will and determination.

Inevitably, what made Buddy great also destroyed him. He might not have reached such heights had he not moved to Europe, but that eventually made him an expatriate American. He might not have burned out so rapidly had he listened to Fred Wilt and been more moderate with his training, but he also might not have burned so brightly. He might have fared better at Tokyo had not his insecurity forced him to push the pace foolishly at Yonkers, but it was not Buddy's nature to let others do the work. Inevitably, our stengths become our weaknesses. Nevertheless, given all of the above, I'm not sure I would have redrawn Buddy's career one step differently.

Buddy feels the same way. When I spoke with him by telephone while writing these words, he sounded cheerful. "I'm happier now than any time in the last 15 years. I'm working three jobs, running every morning, in love with a fine lady. Life couldn't be better."

He was a man ahead of his time. Had there been in 1963 a World Track and Field Championships in the year before the Olympics, as there is now, Buddy certainly would have won the marathon. Although Buddy occasionally received small payments at races, common practice in Europe, he recalls, "the most I ever got was maybe $500 for a race in Brussels." A generation later, ordinary runners receive fees that size with extraordinary runners commanding fees above $100,000. Buddy was extraordinary, but he ran for free, for fun, for glory, on an Olympic quest, accumulating little money, but achieving a fine competitive record. He averaged 43 races each of his first two years in Europe: 10 in cross-country, 10 on the roads and 23 in track.

While researching my article for *The Runner*, I had examined Buddy's diary sheets for the period following Yonkers, a record not of victories, but of a battle with pain and injury. It was enough to make me want to cry. Only in the last month before the Olympics was Buddy able to regain any consistency in training. Considering his problems between the Trials and Games, he ran admirably in Tokyo. His sixth place finish was a testimonial to his strength of mind as much as strength of body.

A half-mile from the stadium, Buddy caught Aurele Vandendriessche, two-time Boston winner. As though the Belgian knew that Americans a quarter century later would remember his name more than that of their own countryman, he turned and smiled as Buddy passed.

Buddy Edelen had many strengths as a runner: his stamina, his perseverance, an iron will, his obsessive-compulsive personality, unquestionably a favorable ratio of slow-twitch fibers. But he also had one fatal flaw, a sciatic nerve condition, that flared at the wrong moment. Fred Wilt had told his athletes, "In every race there comes a critical moment when victory hangs in the balance." So had it been with Buddy. If fate had permitted Leonard Graves Edelen four more months of grace, he might have won that Olympic medal, maybe gold, and people today would not need to ask: "Buddy who?" Who knows how much not only his life, but the history of running, might have been changed.

Bibliography and Acknowledgements

The description of Emil Zatopek's training in Chapter Two is taken from *How They Train,* compiled and written by Fred Wilt, published by *Track and Field News* in 1959. More generally, I referred to Peter Lovesey's book, *Five Kings of Distance*, published in 1981 by St. Martin's Press.

The description of Jim Peters' training in Chapter Two may be found, among other sources, in *The Masters of the Marathon* by Richard Benyo, published by Atheneum in 1983 and in the instructional book *Middle and Long Distance Marathon and Steeplechase* published by the British Amateur Athletic Board, written by D.C.V. Watts and Harry Wilson.

The race summary and splits from the 1952 Olympic Marathon in Helsinki originate with the official report of the British Olympic Association on the Olympic Games of 1952. The report was published by World Sport.

Section III of Chapter Two is written in the first person of Fred Wilt but the words, together with statements of fact and opinion, are those of the writer, the use of first person being a device only. Mr. Wilt bears no responsibility for the statements made therein, all such responsibility being that of the writer.

Abebe Bikila, the subject of Chapter Three, has inspired some of the most lyrical writing in the literature of track and field. Among the sources consulted for this work are : *Olympic Diary, Rome 1960* by Neil Allen, published by Nicholas Kaye, Ltd. in 1960, *The Lonely Breed* by Ron Clarke and Norman Harris, published by Pelham Books in 1967; and *The African Running Revolution,* edited by Dave Prokop, published by World Publications in 1975. The statement of Bikila's training prior to Rome appeared in Mr. Prokop's book in an article written by Mr. Prokop.

For the description of the courses, as well as the historical development of the various marathons in which Buddy Edelen participated, I consulted the following sources: *The Guinness Book of the Marathon* by Roger Gynn, published by Guinness Superlatives, Ltd. in 1984; *The Marathon, The Runners and The Race,* by Norman Giller, first published in the United States by Chartwell Books, a division of Book Sales, Inc. and published in England by Winchmore Publishing Services, Ltd. in 1983; and *The World of Marathons,* by Sandy Treadwell, published by Stewart, Tabori and Chang in 1987. In determining that Buddy Edelen was the first American since 1925 (and not an earlier date) to hold the world best in the marathon, I gave credit to Albert "Whitey" Michelson for his 2:29:01.8, in a marathon that ran from Columbus Circle, New York, to Liberty Square, Port Chester. Mr. Michelson's time was the first under 2:30 for the event. This information is reported in *The Guinness Book of the Marathon* and in the Media Guide to the 1988 United States Olympic Marathon Trial. Some sources, notably *The Marathon,* do not include Mr. Michelson's performance on the developing list of world bests for the event, but I found no basis upon which the performance should be discounted.

I referred for descriptions of the Polytechnic Marathon course, Windsor to Chiswick, to Ron Hill's two volume autobiography, *The Long Hard Road,* published by Ron Hill Sports, Ltd. in 1981.

With regard to the Boston Marathon, I referred not only to the above sources but also to a brochure published by The Boston Globe, with the principal writing done by Jerry Nason of the Globe staff.

The Self-Made Olympian, by Ron Daws, published by World

Publications in 1977, was helpful in reconstructing the 1964 Olympic Trials Marathon in Yonkers, New York.

Leonard Shecter covered the 1964 Olympics as a journalist and later wrote a book entitled *The Jocks,* which featured Buddy Edelen. I referred both to the book and to Mr. Shecter's reporting particularly for description of the 1964 Olympic Marathon and for descriptions of the lifestyle and training that led to that performance. I am also indebted to Mr. Shecter for noticing the changes which occurred as Buddy turned from his school teacher persona to competitive racer.

Generally, I referred throughout this book to the training schedules discussed in Fred Wilt's book, *Run, Run, Run,* published in 1964 by Track and Field News, Inc.

With regard to the description of the 1964 Olympic Trials Marathon, it should be noted that the "stream of consciousness" found in Subsection V does not, of course, represent Buddy Edelen's exact thought process during the run. Rather, the section is designed to illustrate the constant battle a runner has in maintaining associative thinking during a run as long as the marathon and how easily dissociative thinking may occur. The chapter also articulates, by example, the idea that every runner is controlled by two voices, one of which confidently addresses the task at hand and the other of which imagines pain and discomfort with each step. The run itself is the resolution of contradictory internal dialogue. The words belong to the writer as does the full responsibility for content, whether opinion or fact.

In over 20 years of running and reading it is possible that I have retained images first presented by other writers in other works. I have consulted only those mentioned here and am unaware of any other specific sources, to the authors of which I might owe a debt of gratitude and acknowledgment. If I knew who they were, I would have no hesitation in expressing my appreciation.

No acknowledgement would be complete without an expression of gratitude to Fred Wilt, who kindly shared his time with me during a busy season coaching the Purdue University women's team, and to Mr. Wilt's wife, who was a most gracious hostess during my visit to Purdue.

And, finally, thanks are due to Buddy Edelen, who gave his complete cooperation to this project and who inspired, by his nature, the hard work of the many people who brought this book to completion.

The Photographs
Credits

All photographs reproduced in the book are from the private collection of Leonard Graves Edelen, collected over the course of his career and reproduced here with his permission.

Many of the photographs maintained by Mr. Edelen do not show the name of the photographer or agency. The photographs subject to identification are credited as follows, in the order of appearance: Chapter One: Time Life; Reuters; Time Life. Chapter Two: Paul Siegel; Chapter Five: (2) E.D. Lacy, 55 Graham Road, Mitcham, Surrey. Chapter Six: (1) Het Laatste Nieuws Inzender. Chapter Seven: (1) and (2) United Agency Photoreporters. Chapter Sixteen: (1) and (2) Sport and General Press Agency, Ltd., Fleet Street, London. Chapter Seventeen: (2) Foto Hurka. Chapter Eighteen: Time Life. Chapter Nineteen: New York Times. Chapter Twenty: Kelo-Lance Photo, Sioux Falls, South Dakota. Chapter Twenty-five: (1) Keystone Press Agency Ltd., Fleet Street, London. Chapter Twenty-Five (1) and (2) Time Life. Afterword: Steve Pierce, Fort Collins, Colorado.

Frank Murphy

Frank Murphy is a lawyer and the Public Administrator of Jackson County, Missouri. He coaches the men's and women's cross-country teams at Rockhurst College in Kansas City, Missouri.

Hal Higdon

Hal Higdon is a Senior Writer for *Runners World Magazine* and has written many articles and books about running, including *Run Fast*.

About the Book

The text of this book was written in Microsoft Word and designed in Aldus Pagemaker 4.0 on the Macintosh computer.

The body text is set in Caslon 540 and the *italics* set in Berkley Italic.

Book Design and Cover Design by Susan Ng.

Cover illustration by Scott Mack.